The Algorithmic Friend:

How to Build Genuine Connections in a World of
Digital Distractions

Alex Kim

CONTENTS

114

1. Introduction: The Importance of Genuine Connections in a Digital World

1.1 The Power of Connection

The power of connection is one of the most fundamental aspects of human existence. We all crave genuine connections with other people, whether it be in our personal or professional lives. In a world where technology dominates our daily routines, it can be difficult to establish and maintain authentic relationships. With the rise of social media and the prevalence of digital distractions, it is becoming more challenging to build meaningful connections with others. However, the power of connection can never be underestimated, and it is crucial to prioritize genuine relationships in a world of digital noise.

Genuine connections provide us with a sense of belonging, fulfillment, and purpose. They make us feel supported, valued, and understood. They help us to grow and learn from others, and they enrich our lives in countless ways. The power of connection is so great that it can even have a positive impact on our physical health. Studies have shown that people with strong social support systems live longer, healthier lives than those without such connections.

In a world where technology often serves as a substitute for human interaction, it is vital to recognize the importance of genuine connections. It is essential to prioritize face-to-face interactions, to take the time to listen and engage with others, and to build meaningful relationships that are based on mutual trust and respect. The power of connection can help us to navigate life's challenges, to find joy and meaning in our experiences, and to create a sense of community and belonging that transcends the digital world.

1.2 The Changing Landscape of Relationships

The technological advancements in recent years have significantly impacted the way we interact with one another, and more specifically, how we form and maintain relationships. With the rise of social media platforms and dating apps, the traditional methods of forming connections have been replaced with a more digital approach. While this may have made it easier to discover and communicate with new people, it has also changed the landscape of relationships.

In the past, relationships were built on face-to-face communication and shared experiences. Today, relationships can be formed and maintained solely through digital communication. This has resulted in less emphasis on physical proximity and more on shared interests and values. Furthermore, the ease of communication has led to a larger pool of potential partners and friends, which has both positive and negative implications.

On one hand, people can now connect with individuals they may never have met otherwise, creating opportunities for meaningful connections. On the other hand, the abundance of options can lead to a sense of overwhelming choice, making it difficult to commit to any one person or group. Additionally, the lack of physical interaction can make it harder to establish genuine connections and fully understand the nuances of another person's personality.

As the landscape of relationships continues to shift, it is important to consider how technology can both help and hinder our ability to form genuine connections. Understanding the potential pitfalls and benefits of digital communication can help us navigate this evolving terrain and build authentic relationships in a world of digital distractions.

1.3 The Risk of Superficiality

The rise of digital communication has transformed the way we interact with each other. We can now connect with people from all over the world at any time of the day. However, this convenience comes with a risk of superficiality. We might have hundreds or even thousands of friends on social media, but how many of them do we actually know on a personal level? With the ease of liking, commenting, and sharing, we might feel like we are keeping in touch with our friends, but in reality, we are only scratching the surface. Genuine connections require time, effort, and vulnerability, and the algorithmic nature of social media does not always allow for that.

The risk of superficiality is not just limited to online interactions. In our fast-paced world, we are often too busy to invest in meaningful relationships. We might have a large network of acquaintances, but when it comes to true friends, we might find ourselves lacking. We might even prioritize our work or hobbies over our relationships, leaving us feeling disconnected and lonely. The risk of superficiality is not just a digital problem; it is a problem that affects us all.

To build genuine connections, we need to be intentional about our interactions. We need to make time for the people who matter to us and show a genuine interest in their lives. We need to be vulnerable and share our own fears and struggles. We need to listen actively and be present in the moment. Genuine connections cannot be built overnight, but with persistence and effort, they can last a lifetime. By recognizing the risk of superficiality and taking steps to overcome it, we can build meaningful relationships that enrich our lives.

1.4 The Paradox of Technology

The paradox of technology is that while it has connected us to an unprecedented extent, it has also made genuine connections more elusive than ever. With the advent of social media and messaging apps, we are constantly bombarded with notifications, updates, and messages. This endless stream of information can be overwhelming, and it can be hard to find the time and space to truly connect with the people in our lives. Moreover, the ease of communication that technology provides can lead us to take our relationships for granted. We may feel like we are keeping in touch with someone because we send them the occasional message, but this is not the same as truly engaging with them on a deeper level.

Furthermore, social media can create an illusion of connection without actually fostering genuine relationships. We may have hundreds or even thousands of followers or friends on social media, but how many of these people do we actually have meaningful connections with? It is easy to fall into the trap of thinking that likes, comments, and shares are a substitute for the real thing, but this is not the case.

In short, technology can be both a blessing and a curse when it comes to building genuine connections. While it offers us unparalleled opportunities to connect with others, it can also distract us from the people who are right in front of us and create a false sense of intimacy. To truly build genuine connections in a world of digital distractions, we need to be intentional about how we use technology and make a conscious effort to prioritize the relationships that matter most to us.

1.5 The Importance of Balance

The importance of balance cannot be overemphasized in today's world of digital distractions. Many people have become so engrossed in their devices and social media platforms that they forget to strike a balance between their online and offline activities. It is crucial to identify the activities that bring genuine connections and prioritize them while minimizing the less important ones.

Balance is essential to our wellbeing, and it helps us to stay focused and productive. It enables us to prioritize our time and energy and avoid burnout. When we strike a balance between our online and offline activities, we can build meaningful relationships with the people around us, engage in activities that bring us joy and fulfillment, and maintain a healthy lifestyle.

In a world where technology has made it easy to connect with people from different parts of the world, it is essential to maintain genuine connections with the people around us. Balancing our online and offline activities allows us to build and maintain these connections, which are fundamental to our social, emotional, and mental wellbeing.

Therefore, we must learn to prioritize our activities, limit our screen time, and spend more time engaging in activities that enrich our lives. We must learn to disconnect from the digital world and reconnect with ourselves, our families, and our communities. Striking a balance between our digital and real-life activities is critical to building genuine connections and living a fulfilled life.

1.6 The Role of Intentionality

is crucial in building genuine connections in a world of digital distractions. In this fast-paced digital age, we are constantly bombarded with information, notifications, and messages that make it easy to lose sight of what is important – the people around us. The more we rely on technology to connect with others, the more we risk losing the ability to form genuine relationships. Intentionality is the key to creating meaningful connections, and it requires us to be mindful and purposeful in our interactions with others.

Intentionality means taking the time to focus on the person you are interacting with, listening actively to what they have to say, and responding thoughtfully. It is about being present in the moment and showing genuine interest in the other person. When we approach our interactions with intentionality, we create a safe and authentic environment where trust can develop, and meaningful connections can be formed.

Intentionality also involves setting clear boundaries around our use of technology. We need to be mindful of how much time we spend on our devices and how it affects our ability to connect with others.

By setting limits and prioritizing face-to-face interactions, we can cultivate deeper connections and build stronger relationships.

Overall, the role of intentionality is critical in building genuine connections in a world of digital distractions. It requires us to be mindful, purposeful, and present in our interactions with others, and to prioritize human connection over convenience. By embracing intentionality, we can create a more meaningful and fulfilling life, both online and offline.

1.7 The Need for a New Approach

In today's world, we are more connected than ever before. Social media platforms, messaging apps, and various other digital tools are readily available to keep us connected with our friends and family at all times. However, despite the plethora of options, digital connections often lack the depth and authenticity necessary for building genuine relationships. As a result, we are left feeling disconnected and unfulfilled, even when we are surrounded by people online.

The need for a new approach to building connections is clear. In a world dominated by algorithms and digital distractions, it's essential to create intentional spaces for meaningful interactions. We need to prioritize genuine connections over the endless scrolling and mindless tapping that characterize so much of our digital lives.

The key to building genuine connections in a digital world is to approach relationships with intentionality and mindfulness. We must be intentional about how we use digital tools to connect with others, and we must be mindful of the ways in which these tools can both facilitate and hinder genuine connections. By taking a more intentional and mindful approach to building relationships, we can create deeper connections that are more fulfilling and rewarding than those found on social media or other digital platforms.

In short, the need for a new approach to building connections in a digital world is clear. By prioritizing intentionality and mindfulness, we can create genuine connections that are meaningful and fulfilling, even in a world dominated by algorithms and digital distractions.

1.8 The Promise of Algorithmic Friendship

In today's digital age, it is easy to feel disconnected from others, even when we are constantly surrounded by technology that is supposed to connect us. However, there is a promise of algorithmic friendship that can help us build genuine connections with others. Algorithms can be used to connect us with like-minded individuals, help us find new hobbies and interests, and even facilitate offline interactions. By using algorithms to sift through vast amounts of data, we can find people who share our passions and values, making it easier to build long-lasting friendships. Additionally, algorithms can help us break out of our social bubbles, exposing us to new ideas and perspectives. In a world where echo chambers are all too common, this is a valuable tool for building genuine connections that span different backgrounds, cultures, and beliefs.

Of course, this promise of algorithmic friendship also comes with challenges. There is a risk of relying too heavily on technology to build connections, leading to a loss of genuine human interaction. It is important to strike a balance between using technology to facilitate connections and engaging in face-to-face interactions with others. Additionally, algorithms can also perpetuate biases and limit diversity, so it is important to be aware of these issues and actively work to counteract them.

Overall, the promise of algorithmic friendship offers a new way to build genuine connections in a digital world. By using technology to connect us with others and facilitate offline interactions, we can break down barriers and build meaningful relationships that would not have been possible otherwise. However, it is important to approach these connections with intentionality and mindfulness, maintaining a balance between technology and human interaction, and being aware of the potential pitfalls and limitations of algorithms.

2. Building Self-Awareness: Understanding Your Relationship with Technology

2.1 The Impact of Technology on our Lives

The impact of technology on our lives has been enormous, and it has transformed the way we live, work, and interact with others. While technology can be incredibly beneficial and convenient, it has also brought with it a range of challenges and negative consequences. The constantly connected, always-on nature of our digital devices has made it difficult to disconnect from work and other responsibilities, leading to increased stress and burnout. Additionally, the constant stimulation of social media and other online platforms has led to decreased attention spans and difficulty focusing on important tasks.

Furthermore, technology has also affected our relationships with others. While it has made it easier to connect with people across the globe, it has also made it more difficult to establish meaningful, in-person connections. Social media and other digital platforms have made it easy to curate an idealized version of ourselves, leading to feelings of inadequacy and insecurity when comparing ourselves to others.

It is important to recognize the impact that technology has on our lives and to develop healthy habits and boundaries around its use. This includes setting limits on technology use, prioritizing in-person relationships, and practicing mindfulness to combat the constant distractions of the digital world. By building self-awareness and understanding our relationship with technology, we can develop a healthier and more balanced approach to its use and create more meaningful connections with those around us.

2.2 The Value of Self-Awareness

The value of self-awareness cannot be emphasized enough, especially in the context of technology. Being self-aware means having a deep understanding of one's own thoughts, emotions, and behaviors. It involves being able to recognize the impact of technology on our lives and understanding how we use it. Self-awareness also means being aware of our own limitations and biases when it comes to technology. By understanding our relationship with technology, we can make intentional and informed decisions about how we use it.

Furthermore, self-awareness helps us to be more mindful of our own habits and patterns. It allows us to recognize when we are being overly reliant on technology or when we are using it in a way that is not beneficial to our well-being. When we are more self-aware, we are better equipped to make changes and adjust our behavior accordingly.

In addition, self-awareness can help us to build more genuine connections with others, even in a world of digital distractions. By understanding how technology is impacting our relationships, we can make intentional choices about how we connect with others. We can prioritize face-to-face interactions and limit our use of technology when it interferes with our ability to connect with others on a deeper level.

Overall, self-awareness is a crucial skill for navigating the complex world of technology. It allows us to be more intentional about how we use technology and helps us to build more genuine connections with others. By understanding our own relationship with technology, we can make informed decisions that benefit our own well-being and the well-being of those around us.

2.3 Identifying Your Relationship with Technology

Identifying your relationship with technology is essential in today's highly connected world. Technology has become an integral part of our lives, and it has revolutionized the way we communicate, work, and live. However, technology can also be a source of distraction and addiction, leading to negative impacts on our well-being and relationships. Therefore, it is crucial to understand our relationship with technology to gain self-awareness and make conscious decisions about our usage patterns.

To identify your relationship with technology, you need to reflect on your behaviors, habits, and emotions related to technology. Ask yourself questions such as: How often do I check my phone? Do I feel anxious or restless when I am away from my devices? Do I prioritize my digital life over my real-life interactions? Do I use technology to escape from reality or cope with stress? Your answers will reveal your tendencies and motivations towards technology and help you recognize any problematic patterns.

It is also essential to consider the impact of technology on your mental and physical health, productivity, and relationships. Are you spending too much time on social media or gaming, leading to sleep deprivation or neglecting your responsibilities? Are you missing out on meaningful connections and real-life experiences because of your digital distractions? Being honest with yourself and acknowledging the consequences of your technology use can motivate you to make positive changes and cultivate a healthier relationship with technology.

In conclusion, identifying your relationship with technology is the first step towards building self-awareness and creating a balanced and fulfilling life in the digital age. By understanding your motivations, habits, and impacts, you can make conscious choices and use technology as a tool for connection, learning, and creativity, rather than a source of addiction and stress.

2.4 Exploring Your Digital Habits

Exploring your digital habits is essential for developing self-awareness and understanding your relationship with technology. With the proliferation of digital devices and platforms in our lives, it is easy to become unaware of how much time we spend on them and how they impact our daily routines. Taking time to reflect on your digital habits can provide valuable insight into your behavior, values, and priorities.

Start by examining how you use technology throughout the day. Do you wake up and immediately check your phone, or do you make a conscious effort to spend some time without it? How often do you check social media or email, and for how long? Do you find yourself mindlessly scrolling through news feeds or watching videos for hours on end? What triggers you to use technology, and how does it make you feel?

As you begin to answer these questions, you may notice patterns emerging. Perhaps you use technology to alleviate boredom or anxiety, or to stay connected with friends and family. You may also recognize that certain apps or platforms are more addictive and time-consuming than others. This awareness can help you make intentional choices about how you use technology and set boundaries that align with your values and goals.

Exploring your digital habits is a valuable tool for building self-awareness and developing a healthy relationship with technology. By examining your behavior and reflecting on how it makes you feel, you can make intentional choices about how you use technology and create a more balanced and fulfilling life.

2.5 Understanding Your Triggers

Understanding your triggers is a crucial step towards building self-awareness and developing healthier habits around technology. Triggers are the external or internal cues that prompt you to use technology. For example, a notification on your phone, boredom, stress, or anxiety can all be triggers that lead you to check your email or social media. Once you identify your triggers, you can start to take control of your behavior and make conscious decisions about your tech use.

It's important to note that triggers can be positive or negative. Positive triggers might include using technology to connect with friends and family or to pursue a hobby or passion. Negative triggers might include using technology to escape negative emotions or to procrastinate on a task you don't want to do. Understanding both types of triggers can help you develop a balanced relationship with technology.

To identify your triggers, start by paying attention to your behavior around technology. Notice when you feel compelled to check your phone or open a particular app. Ask yourself what emotions or situations might be contributing to your behavior. It can also be helpful to keep a journal or log of your tech use to track patterns and identify triggers.

Once you've identified your triggers, you can start to experiment with different strategies for managing them. For example, if you find that stress is a trigger for excessive tech use, you might try practicing mindfulness or breathing exercises to manage stress instead. If social media is a trigger for procrastination or comparison, you might try limiting your time on those platforms or unfollowing accounts that make you feel bad about yourself. By understanding your triggers and experimenting with different strategies for managing them, you can develop a healthier and more intentional relationship with technology.

2.6 Recognizing the Consequences of Technology Use

Recognizing the consequences of technology use is an essential step in building self-awareness and understanding one's relationship with technology. While technology offers many benefits, such as increased productivity, communication, and entertainment, it can also have negative consequences on our mental and physical health, relationships, and overall well-being. For example, excessive use of social media can lead to feelings of anxiety, loneliness, and depression, as well as a decrease in face-to-face social interactions. Additionally, constantly being connected to technology can lead to a lack of sleep, eye strain, and poor posture.

It is important to recognize these consequences and reflect on how our technology use is affecting our lives. By doing so, we can make conscious decisions about when and how we use technology, and establish healthy boundaries and habits. For example, we might choose to limit our social media use to a certain time of day, or turn off our phones during meal times or before bed. We might also prioritize face-to-face interactions with friends and family, rather than relying solely on digital communication.

Recognizing the consequences of technology use also requires us to think critically about the ways in which technology is designed and how it impacts our society as a whole. We can question the algorithms and data collection practices that shape our online experiences, and advocate for more ethical and responsible technology use. By taking a proactive approach to understanding and managing our relationship with technology, we can build genuine connections and lead more fulfilling lives in a world of digital distractions.

2.7 Assessing Your Digital Well-Being

is an important step towards understanding your relationship with technology. In today's world, we are constantly surrounded by digital distractions, and it can be challenging to strike a balance between our online and offline lives. However, taking the time to reflect on your digital habits and how they impact your overall well-being is crucial for maintaining a healthy relationship with technology.

To assess your digital well-being, it's important to ask yourself a few key questions. Firstly, how much time do you spend on your devices each day? Are you constantly checking your phone, even when you don't need to? Secondly, how does your digital usage affect your mood and emotions? Do you feel anxious or stressed when you're away from your devices? Thirdly, how does your digital usage impact your relationships with others? Are you able to be fully present when you're spending time with friends and family, or do you find yourself constantly checking your phone?

By reflecting on these questions, you can gain a better understanding of your digital habits and how they impact your overall well-being. From there, you can start to make small changes to improve your relationship with technology, such as setting time limits on your phone or taking breaks from social media.

Ultimately, assessing your digital well-being is an ongoing process. It requires continued self-reflection and a willingness to make changes when necessary. However, by building a healthier relationship with technology, you can free up more time and energy to connect with others and engage in the world around you.

2.8 The Benefits of Building Self-Awareness

The benefits of building self-awareness cannot be overstated. Self-awareness is the foundation of emotional intelligence and is the first step towards understanding ourselves and our relationship with technology. When we are self-aware, we are better able to recognize our own emotions, thoughts, and behaviors. This allows us to make more conscious decisions about how we interact with technology and how it affects our lives.

By building self-awareness, we can also improve our communication and relationships with others. When we understand ourselves better, we are better able to empathize with others and recognize their emotions and needs. This allows us to build stronger and more meaningful relationships, both online and offline.

In addition, self-awareness can also help us manage stress and improve our overall well-being. By recognizing our own stress triggers and patterns, we can develop coping strategies and take steps to reduce stress in our lives. This can lead to improved physical health, mental health, and overall happiness.

Finally, building self-awareness can also lead to personal growth and development. When we understand ourselves better, we are better able to identify areas for improvement and work towards becoming our best selves. This can lead to a greater sense of purpose and fulfillment in our lives.

Overall, the benefits of building self-awareness are numerous and far-reaching. By taking the time to understand ourselves and our relationship with technology, we can live more intentional and fulfilling lives in a world of digital distractions.

2.9 Strategies for Developing Self-Awareness

Developing self-awareness is a crucial component of building genuine connections in a world of digital distractions.

Self-awareness is the ability to recognize and understand one's own emotions, thoughts, and behaviors. In order to develop self-awareness, it is important to engage in self-reflection and introspection. One way to do this is through mindfulness practices, such as meditation or journaling. Mindfulness allows us to observe our thoughts and emotions without judgment, which can help us identify patterns and triggers that may be affecting our relationship with technology.

Another strategy for developing self-awareness is to seek feedback from others. This can be done through open and honest communication with friends, family, or even coworkers. It is important to be receptive to feedback and to use it as an opportunity for growth and self-improvement. Additionally, seeking out diverse perspectives and experiences can broaden our understanding of ourselves and others.

Setting goals and tracking progress can also aid in developing self-awareness. By setting specific, measurable, achievable, relevant, and time-bound (SMART) goals related to our relationship with technology, we can better understand our behaviors and motivations. Tracking progress allows us to monitor our growth and adjust our approach as needed.

Finally, seeking professional help from a therapist or counselor can be beneficial in developing self-awareness. A trained professional can provide guidance and support as we navigate our relationship with technology and cultivate greater self-awareness. Ultimately, developing self-awareness is an ongoing process that requires dedication and effort, but the rewards of deeper connections and greater self-understanding are well worth it.

2.10 Conclusion: Moving Forward with Intention and Awareness

In conclusion, building self-awareness and understanding our relationship with technology is crucial in creating genuine connections in the digital world. While technology has brought us many benefits, it has also caused serious problems, such as addiction, mental health issues, and social isolation. It is essential to use technology with intention and awareness, rather than letting it control our lives.

To move forward, we need to practice mindfulness and self-reflection. We must ask ourselves why we use technology and what purpose it serves in our lives. We need to be aware of the impact technology has on our emotions, thoughts, and behavior. When we are mindful of our relationship with technology, we can identify the negative effects it has on us and take steps to manage them.

Moreover, we need to be aware of the algorithms that govern our online experiences. Algorithms are designed to keep us engaged and addicted, and they can manipulate our behavior without our knowledge. By understanding how algorithms work, we can take control of our online experiences and use technology in a way that benefits us.

In short, building self-awareness and understanding our relationship with technology is a continuous process that requires effort and mindfulness. However, it is essential for creating genuine connections and living a fulfilling life in the digital world. By using technology with intention and awareness, we can build stronger relationships, increase our well-being, and lead more meaningful lives.

3. Reclaiming Your Attention: Strategies for Digital Minimalism

3.1 The Problem with Digital Distractions

In today's digital age, we are constantly bombarded with notifications, messages, and updates, all vying for our attention. While technology has made our lives easier and more efficient in many ways, it has also created a major problem - digital distractions. The constant lure of social media, email, and other digital distractions can have a detrimental effect on our productivity, concentration, and overall well-being.

One of the biggest problems with digital distractions is that they pull us away from the present moment. We may be physically present in a meeting, at dinner with friends, or spending time with family, but mentally we are elsewhere, scrolling through our social media feeds or checking our email. This not only makes it difficult for us to fully engage with the people around us, but it also robs us of the opportunity to fully experience and enjoy the moment.

Another problem with digital distractions is that they can lead to a constant state of information overload. We are inundated with so much information on a daily basis that it can be difficult to filter out what's important and what's not. This can lead to feelings of overwhelm, anxiety, and stress, which can have a negative impact on our mental health and well-being.

To combat these issues, it's important to develop strategies for digital minimalism. This means taking a step back from technology and being more intentional about how we use it. This may involve setting limits on our social media use, turning off notifications, and carving out designated times for checking email or browsing the internet. By doing so, we can reclaim our attention and focus on what truly matters - building genuine connections with the people around us.

3.2 The Benefits of Digital Minimalism

The benefits of digital minimalism are many and varied. At the most basic level, digital minimalism allows us to reclaim our attention from the constant barrage of notifications and distractions that pervade our lives. By intentionally limiting our use of technology, we can reduce the amount of time we spend on mindless activities that add little value to our lives, and focus instead on what truly matters. This can include spending more time with loved ones, pursuing hobbies and interests, or simply taking time to reflect and recharge.

In addition to these immediate benefits, digital minimalism can also have a profound impact on our mental and emotional well-being. By reducing our exposure to the constant stress and anxiety that often accompany our digital lives, we can experience a greater sense of peace and calm. This can lead to improved sleep, reduced anxiety, and greater overall happiness and well-being.

Finally, digital minimalism can also help us to build more meaningful and genuine connections with others. By reducing the amount of time we spend on social media and other digital platforms, we can focus more on face-to-face interactions and genuine conversations. This can help us to forge deeper connections with those around us, and to build a more authentic and fulfilling social life.

Overall, the benefits of digital minimalism are clear: by intentionally limiting our use of technology, we can reclaim our attention, improve our mental and emotional well-being, and build more meaningful connections with others. If you're feeling overwhelmed by the constant noise and distraction of the digital world, it may be time to consider adopting a more minimalist approach to your technology use.

3.3 Identifying Digital Clutter in Your Life

Digital clutter refers to the excess of digital information, notifications, and distractions that interfere with our ability to focus and be productive. It encompasses the accumulation of unused apps, unread emails, and unnecessary social media notifications that have a profound impact on our mental health and wellbeing. Identifying digital clutter in our lives is the first step towards building a more meaningful and authentic relationship with technology. To do so, we need to be intentional about the digital tools we use and their purpose in our lives.

One effective way to identify digital clutter is to conduct a digital audit. A digital audit involves taking inventory of all the digital tools we use, including social media accounts, email, messaging apps, and productivity tools. We should then evaluate each tool's relevance to our lives, its usefulness, and its impact on our attention and productivity. It is essential to determine the tools that serve a valuable purpose in our lives and those that contribute to digital clutter.

Another way to identify digital clutter is to pay attention to the notifications we receive. Notifications are a significant source of distraction and can negatively impact our attention and focus. We can reduce digital clutter by turning off notifications for unnecessary apps and social media accounts. This step allows us to prioritize the notifications that matter and reduce the noise that interferes with our mental clarity.

In conclusion, identifying digital clutter in our lives requires intentional evaluation of our digital tools and the notifications we receive. By doing so, we can create a more mindful and purposeful approach to digital technology and build a more meaningful relationship with it.

3.4 The Importance of Unplugging

In today's digital age, it's easy to get caught up in the never-ending cycle of notifications, emails, social media updates, and other forms of digital noise. But amidst all of these distractions, it's becoming increasingly important to unplug and take a break from technology. This is particularly true when it comes to building genuine connections with others.

When we're constantly plugged in, we're not fully present in the moment. We might be physically present with someone, but our minds are elsewhere, scrolling through our phones or checking our email. This can make it difficult to truly connect with others and build genuine relationships.

By unplugging, we give ourselves the opportunity to be fully present in the moment. We can focus on the people we're with, engage in meaningful conversations, and build stronger connections with those around us. Additionally, unplugging can help us recharge and rejuvenate, allowing us to be more productive and focused when we do eventually return to our devices.

It's important to note that unplugging doesn't have to mean disconnecting completely. We can still stay connected to the people and things that matter most to us, but we can do so on our own terms. By setting boundaries around our use of technology, we can ensure that we're using it in a way that supports our goals and values, rather than letting it control us.

Overall, the importance of unplugging cannot be overstated. By taking regular breaks from technology, we can prioritize our relationships and build deeper connections with the people around us. So the next time you find yourself scrolling mindlessly through your phone, consider taking a break and unplugging for a while. You might be surprised by how much more present and engaged you feel.

3.5 Creating a Digital Sanctuary

Creating a digital sanctuary refers to the deliberate practice of carving out time and space for uninterrupted, technology-free activities. In a world where we are constantly bombarded with notifications and alerts, it can be challenging to disconnect and enjoy moments of stillness. However, research has shown that such moments are crucial for our mental health and well-being. Creating a digital sanctuary can help us achieve a sense of balance and mindfulness in our digital lives.

To create a digital sanctuary, it's important to start small. Begin by designating a specific time of day or week where you disconnect from technology completely. This can be as simple as turning off your phone for an hour a day or going for a walk without any devices. The key is to create a routine that works for you and can be easily maintained.

Another way to create a digital sanctuary is by setting boundaries around your digital devices. This could mean setting limits on social media usage or disabling notifications during certain times of the day. By taking control of how and when you engage with technology, you can create more space for quiet reflection and focus.

Finally, creating a physical space that is free from digital distractions can also be helpful. This could be a quiet corner in your home or office where you can read or meditate without any interruptions. The act of physically distancing yourself from technology can help you feel more present and mindful in the moment.

Overall, creating a digital sanctuary requires intentionality and discipline. However, the benefits of disconnecting and creating space for stillness and reflection are well worth the effort. By reclaiming our attention and building healthy habits around technology, we can cultivate deeper, more meaningful connections with ourselves and others.

3.6 The Power of Single-Tasking

In our fast-paced, technology-driven world, multitasking has become the norm. We are constantly checking emails, scrolling through social media, and responding to notifications while working on other tasks. However, research has shown that multitasking can actually decrease productivity and lead to increased stress levels. This is where the power of single-tasking comes in.

Single-tasking is the practice of focusing on one task at a time without any distractions. By giving our undivided attention to one task, we are able to complete it more efficiently and effectively. This allows us to move on to the next task with a clear mind and sense of accomplishment.

In addition to increasing productivity, single-tasking also has mental health benefits. It can reduce stress levels and improve our ability to focus and concentrate. When we are constantly multitasking, our brain is flooded with information and stimuli, which can lead to mental exhaustion and burnout.

To incorporate single-tasking into our daily routine, we need to set boundaries and eliminate distractions. This may mean turning off notifications on our devices or setting specific times to check emails or social media. We should also prioritize our tasks and focus on the most important ones first, rather than trying to tackle everything at once.

In a world where we are constantly bombarded with digital distractions, the power of single-tasking can help us reclaim our attention and increase our productivity and mental wellbeing.

3.7 The Role of Mindfulness in Digital Minimalism

The practice of mindfulness has gained immense popularity in recent years, primarily due to the increasing levels of stress and anxiety that people experience in their daily lives. Mindfulness refers to an individual's ability to be fully present and aware of their thoughts, feelings, and surroundings. It involves paying attention to the present moment and observing one's thoughts and emotions without judgment. The role of mindfulness in digital minimalism is significant as it can help individuals become more intentional and aware of their digital consumption habits.

By practicing mindfulness, individuals can become more conscious of how they use technology and the impact it has on their lives. It can help them identify triggers that lead to mindless scrolling and distractions, allowing them to develop strategies to overcome these challenges. Mindfulness can also help individuals become more focused and productive, allowing them to prioritize their goals and objectives.

Moreover, mindfulness can help individuals develop a more profound appreciation for their offline connections and relationships. By being fully present and engaged in their interactions with others, individuals can strengthen their connections, leading to a more fulfilling and satisfying life.

In essence, the role of mindfulness in digital minimalism is to help individuals cultivate a more deliberate and intentional relationship with technology. By practicing mindfulness, individuals can develop greater self-awareness, enabling them to make conscious choices about their digital consumption habits. Ultimately, the practice of mindfulness can help individuals reclaim their attention and build more meaningful connections in a world dominated by digital distractions.

3.8 Implementing Digital Minimalism in Your Life

The first step in implementing digital minimalism in your life is to take stock of your digital tools and assess their impact on your attention and well-being. Start by identifying the apps and websites that you use regularly, and ask yourself whether they add value to your life or simply serve as distractions. Be honest with yourself about the amount of time and attention that you devote to digital activities, and consider setting limits on your usage to create space for more meaningful activities.

Once you have identified the tools and activities that are most important to you, focus on cultivating intentional and mindful relationships with them. This may mean setting aside specific times of day for checking email or social media, or turning off notifications and scheduling regular breaks to disconnect from your devices. Be deliberate about the technology that you choose to use, and seek out tools that support your values and goals rather than simply adding to the noise.

Above all, remember that digital minimalism is not about disconnecting entirely from the digital world, but rather about using technology in a deliberate and intentional way that supports your well-being and allows you to focus on what really matters. By being intentional about the role that technology plays in your life, you can reclaim your attention and build genuine connections with the people and activities that are most meaningful to you.

3.9 Overcoming FOMO and Other Digital Temptations

Overcoming FOMO and other digital temptations is crucial for anyone who wants to build genuine connections in a world of digital distractions. FOMO, or Fear of Missing Out, is a powerful force that can lead us to spend hours scrolling through social media feeds or checking our email inboxes obsessively, even when we know deep down that there's nothing truly meaningful or important waiting for us there.

To overcome FOMO, we need to recognize that our time and attention are finite resources that we must use wisely. We need to be intentional about how we spend our time online, setting clear goals and priorities for ourselves and focusing on the activities that truly matter to us. This may mean cutting back on social media use or logging out of email and other distracting apps during certain times of the day.

Other digital temptations, such as the constant stream of notifications and alerts that can interrupt our focus and pull us away from the present moment, also require intentional management. We can turn off unnecessary notifications, set boundaries around our use of technology, and cultivate mindfulness and awareness to help us resist the urge to constantly check our devices.

Ultimately, overcoming FOMO and other digital temptations requires a commitment to living a more intentional and mindful life. By understanding the power of our own attention and taking control of how we use it, we can build stronger connections with others, cultivate deeper meaning and purpose in our lives, and live more fully in the present moment.

3.10 The Impact of Digital Minimalism on Your Relationships

In today's world, social media platforms and other digital distractions have made it difficult to maintain genuine, fulfilling relationships with others. However, the concept of digital minimalism can help us to focus more on our relationships and improve them. By limiting our screen time and social media usage, we can free up more time for face-to-face interactions and quality time with our loved ones.

Digital minimalism can also help us to be more present in our relationships. When we are constantly checking our phones or scrolling through social media, we are not fully present in the moment with the people around us. By minimizing our digital distractions, we can be more attentive and engaged in our relationships, which can lead to deeper connections and more meaningful interactions.

Another way that digital minimalism can impact our relationships is by reducing the pressure to constantly compare ourselves to others. Social media can often make us feel like we are not living up to certain expectations, which can negatively impact our self-esteem and relationships. By limiting our exposure to social media, we can focus more on our own lives and relationships, rather than constantly comparing ourselves to others.

Overall, digital minimalism can have a positive impact on our relationships by allowing us to be more present, attentive, and engaged with the people around us. By taking steps to reduce our digital distractions, we can foster deeper connections and enjoy more fulfilling relationships with our loved ones.

4. The Science of Connection: How Relationships Form and Flourish

4.1 The Dynamics of Connection: How Relationships Work

The dynamics of connection refer to the various factors that influence the formation and maintenance of relationships. One of the key factors that determine how relationships work is communication. Effective communication involves both verbal and non-verbal cues, active listening, and empathetic understanding. In today's digital age, technology has provided us with numerous platforms for communication, but it has also made it easier to misinterpret messages due to the lack of physical cues such as tone of voice and body language.

Trust is another important factor in the dynamics of connection. Trust is built over time and is often based on shared experiences and consistent behavior. It is also critical to be authentic and transparent in relationships, as being genuine creates a sense of safety and comfort in communication.

Another factor that influences how relationships work is the level of emotional intimacy shared between individuals. Emotional intimacy is the ability to be vulnerable and open with another person, sharing deep emotions and feelings. This level of intimacy can be challenging to achieve, but it is essential for building genuine connections and meaningful relationships.

Finally, the dynamics of connection also involve the concept of reciprocity. Reciprocity refers to the mutual exchange of support, trust, and respect between individuals. It is essential in relationships because it creates a sense of balance and equality, which is necessary for the sustainability of any relationship.

Overall, the dynamics of connection are complex and multifaceted. They involve various factors such as communication, trust, emotional intimacy, and reciprocity. By understanding these dynamics, individuals can build genuine connections in a world of digital distractions and foster relationships that are meaningful and fulfilling.

4.2 Oxytocin and Connection: The Role of Neurochemistry in Building Bonds

Oxytocin is a hormone that plays a significant role in forming and maintaining social bonds. Dubbed as the "love hormone," oxytocin is released during intimate physical contact, such as hugging, kissing, and sex. It strengthens social connections by reducing anxiety and promoting trust and empathy. Oxytocin is also associated with maternal behavior, as it promotes the bonding between mother and child during breastfeeding and childbirth. In addition, studies have shown that oxytocin levels increase during positive social interactions, such as sharing personal stories, laughing, and even just looking into someone's eyes.

Research has also suggested that oxytocin may play a role in romantic relationships. Couples who reported higher levels of oxytocin had stronger emotional bonds and reported greater relationship satisfaction. Oxytocin may also play a role in the formation of friendships, as individuals who reported higher levels of oxytocin had more social support and greater feelings of belonging.

In today's world of digital distractions, it is important to acknowledge the role of neurochemistry in building bonds. While technology has made it easier to connect with others, it may also lead to a lack of intimacy and emotional connection. Therefore, it is important to prioritize face-to-face interactions and physical touch to promote the release of oxytocin and strengthen social bonds. By understanding the role of oxytocin in forming and maintaining relationships, we can take intentional steps to build genuine connections in a world that is increasingly disconnected.

4.3 Attachment Theory: Understanding How Our Early Relationships Shape Our Connections Today

Attachment theory proposes that the relationship we have with our primary caregiver in early childhood creates a blueprint for how we connect with others in adulthood. This theory suggests that the relationship we have with our caregiver influences our emotional, behavioral and social development, and informs how we interact with others throughout our lives. There are three types of attachment styles that are typically identified: secure attachment, ambivalent attachment, and avoidant attachment.

Secure attachment is associated with individuals who received consistent and nurturing care from their caregiver. These individuals tend to be comfortable with closeness, express their emotions easily, and have healthy relationships based on mutual trust and respect. In contrast, ambivalent attachment occurs when a caregiver provides inconsistent care, leading an individual to become anxious and uncertain about the availability of love and support from others. This type of attachment can lead to difficulties in forming and maintaining relationships, and may lead to a tendency to cling to others. Avoidant attachment occurs when a caregiver is emotionally unavailable, leading an individual to develop a tendency to avoid emotional connection and closeness with others.

Understanding attachment theory can provide insights into how our early relationships shape our current connections. By recognizing our attachment style, we can work towards developing a secure attachment style if it is not already present. This can involve identifying and addressing any unresolved issues or traumas related to our early attachment experiences, as well as practicing healthy communication and boundary-setting skills in our current relationships. Incorporating these skills into our interactions can lead to healthier and more fulfilling connections with others, both online and offline.

4.4 The Power of Vulnerability: How Sharing Our True Selves Deepens Relationships

The power of vulnerability cannot be overstated in deepening our relationships with others. When we share our true selves, we create a space for others to do the same, and this reciprocal sharing can lead to profound connections. In a world where social media encourages us to curate and present only the most polished versions of ourselves, vulnerability can feel scary and uncomfortable. But it is precisely in those moments of discomfort that we have the opportunity to connect more deeply with others.

When we allow ourselves to be vulnerable, we signal to others that we trust them and value their opinion. This creates a sense of intimacy and closeness that is difficult to replicate in other ways. Additionally, vulnerability can help us to navigate conflict and difficult emotions in our relationships. By being open and honest about our feelings, we can work through misunderstandings and come to a deeper understanding of one another.

Of course, vulnerability can also be risky. It requires us to let go of our need for control and to expose our flaws and imperfections. But when we take that risk, we often find that others are more accepting and compassionate than we anticipated. By embracing vulnerability, we can create more authentic and meaningful relationships in a world that often encourages us to hide our true selves.

4.5 The Importance of Trust: Building and Maintaining Strong Connections

The importance of trust in building and maintaining strong connections cannot be overstated. Trust is the foundation of any healthy relationship, and without it, it is difficult for connections to form, let alone flourish. In fact, studies have shown that trust is the most important factor in establishing a close and meaningful relationship. When we trust someone, we feel safe and secure in their presence, and we are more likely to open up and share our thoughts and feelings with them.

Building trust takes time and effort, and it requires a willingness to be vulnerable and authentic. It also requires consistency and reliability, as well as a willingness to communicate openly and honestly. When we demonstrate these qualities in our interactions with others, we create a sense of safety and security that makes it easier for them to trust us in return.

Maintaining trust is equally important, and it requires ongoing effort and attention. We must be mindful of our words and actions, and we must be willing to listen and respond to the needs of others. When we make mistakes or break trust, we must take responsibility for our actions and work to repair the damage that has been done.

In today's world of digital distractions, building and maintaining trust can be particularly challenging. Social media and other digital platforms can create a false sense of connection, and it can be tempting to rely on these tools to build relationships. However, true connection requires more than just a few likes or comments. It requires a willingness to invest time and energy in building real, meaningful connections with others.

In conclusion, trust is essential for building and maintaining strong connections. It requires authenticity, vulnerability, consistency, and communication. In a world of digital distractions, it is more important than ever to prioritize genuine connection over superficial interactions. By doing so, we can build relationships that are meaningful, fulfilling, and long-lasting.

4.6 Shared Experiences: Creating Memories and Strengthening Relationships

Shared experiences are a vital component of building and strengthening relationships. When we experience something together, we create a memory that we can share and reflect on.

These memories help to bond us and create a sense of connection that can last a lifetime. Shared experiences can take many forms, from traveling to a new place, trying a new activity, or simply enjoying a meal together. The key is that it is something that is experienced together, allowing us to see each other in a different light and create a deeper understanding of who we are.

In today's world of digital distractions, it can be easy to overlook the importance of shared experiences. We may think that we are connecting with others through social media or messaging apps, but these interactions lack the depth and nuance of real-world experiences. By prioritizing shared experiences, we can create stronger relationships that are built on a foundation of genuine connection.

Creating opportunities for shared experiences doesn't have to be complicated or expensive. It can be as simple as planning a picnic in the park, going for a hike, or trying a new recipe together. The key is to be present in the moment and fully engage with the experience. By doing so, we can create memories that will last a lifetime and strengthen our relationships with others.

In conclusion, shared experiences are a fundamental part of building and strengthening relationships. In a world where digital distractions can often get in the way, prioritizing real-world experiences can help us to build deeper connections with others. Whether it's trying a new activity or simply spending time together, the memories we create through shared experiences can help to foster a sense of connection and belonging that is essential for a fulfilling life.

4.7 The Role of Social Support: How Our Networks Help Us Thrive

Social support is a fundamental aspect of human life that plays a significant role in our well-being and happiness. Our social networks provide a range of emotional, practical, and informational support that helps us navigate life's challenges and achieve our goals. Indeed, research has consistently shown that individuals with strong social networks tend to be happier, healthier, and more resilient than those who lack such networks.

The benefits of social support can be seen across a range of domains. For example, social support can help us cope with stress by providing emotional comfort and practical assistance. It can also increase our sense of belonging and connectedness, which is important for our mental health and overall well-being. Social support can also provide us with opportunities for personal growth and development by offering feedback, advice, and encouragement.

One of the key functions of social support is to help us regulate our emotions. When under stress or facing difficult situations, our social networks provide us with a safe and supportive environment to vent our feelings, seek advice, or simply receive comfort. This can help us avoid negative coping strategies such as substance abuse or avoidance, which can exacerbate our problems instead of solving them.

In conclusion, social support is an essential component of human life that enables us to thrive in a world of digital distractions. By building genuine connections with others, we can reap the many benefits of social support and achieve our full potential as individuals. Whether through online communities or face-to-face interactions, our social networks provide us with the resources we need to navigate life's challenges and find meaning and purpose in our lives.

4.8 The Impact of Technology on Relationships: Navigating the Good and the Bad

The impact of technology on relationships is undeniable. On the one hand, technology has made it easier than ever to connect with people from all over the world. It has also made it easier to stay in touch with friends and family members who live far away. However, technology has also had some negative effects on relationships. For example, some people rely too heavily on social media to communicate with their loved ones, which can lead to a lack of face-to-face interaction. This can make it difficult to build and maintain meaningful relationships.

Another negative effect of technology on relationships is the constant distraction it provides. With so many apps and notifications vying for our attention, it can be difficult to focus on the people in our lives. This can lead to a feeling of disconnection and detachment from others. Additionally, technology can make it easier to engage in toxic behavior, such as cyberbullying or online harassment. This can be especially damaging to relationships, as it can erode trust and create a sense of fear or anxiety.

Despite these challenges, it is possible to navigate the good and the bad of technology in relationships. One way to do this is to set boundaries around technology use. For example, you could designate certain times of day as "tech-free" zones, or agree to put your phones away during meals or important conversations. It is also important to prioritize face-to-face interaction whenever possible, as this can help to strengthen our connections with others. Finally, it is important to remember that technology is a tool, and that it is up to us to use it in a way that enhances our relationships rather than detracts from them.

4.9 The Dark Side of Social Media: The Link Between Technology and Loneliness

The rise of social media has brought a new dimension to our social lives, but it has also unleashed an unanticipated side effect: loneliness. Social media platforms offer us the opportunity to connect with people from all parts of the world, share our experiences, and stay updated on the latest trends. However, this constant exposure to the world also creates a feeling of loneliness and disconnection. The more time we spend online, the more isolated we become.

The paradox of social media is that while it is designed to connect us, it often has the opposite effect. We have become so dependent on our devices that we are losing the ability to communicate face-to-face. Instead, we spend hours scrolling through feeds and liking posts, which can lead to a sense of emptiness and disengagement. In fact, studies have shown that people who spend more time on social media feel more lonely, depressed, and anxious.

The problem with social media is that it presents a distorted version of reality. We see only the highlight reel of people's lives, and this can create unrealistic expectations and feelings of inadequacy. It is easy to feel left out or excluded when we see others having fun without us, and this can lead to further isolation.

The solution is not to abandon social media altogether, but rather to use it mindfully. We need to be aware of the detrimental effects of social media on our mental health and take steps to mitigate them. This means setting boundaries, limiting our screen time, and seeking out meaningful connections offline. By doing so, we can use social media to enhance our relationships rather than detract from them.

4.10 The Influence of Algorithms: How Technology Shapes Our Connections

In today's digital age, algorithms are an integral part of our lives. They shape our online experience, from the ads we see on social media to the search results we receive on Google. But algorithms also have a significant impact on our connections with others. Social media algorithms have the power to control what we see and who we interact with, influencing who we form relationships with online. These algorithms prioritize content that is popular and engaging, leading us to engage with a select group of people and content. This can create echo chambers, where we are only exposed to ideas and opinions that align with our own.

Furthermore, algorithms can affect our offline relationships as well. Dating apps use algorithms to match individuals based on their interests and preferences. This can make it easier to find a compatible partner, but it can also limit our exposure to new and different people. Additionally, the constant notifications and distractions from our devices can hinder our ability to form genuine connections with others in real life.

However, it's not all negative. Algorithms can also be used to foster connection and community online. For instance, Facebook groups use algorithms to connect people with similar interests and allow them to engage in meaningful conversations. Similarly, online forums and message boards can bring people together to share knowledge and support each other.

Overall, the influence of algorithms on our connections is complex and multifaceted. While they can limit our exposure to new people and ideas, they also offer the potential to bring people together and foster meaningful relationships. As we navigate the digital landscape, it's important to be mindful of the role algorithms play and how they shape our online and offline connections.

4.11 The Future of Connection: Emerging Technologies and New Possibilities

The future of connection is rapidly evolving with the emergence of new technologies and possibilities. The rise of artificial intelligence (AI) and the internet of things (IoT) are transforming the way we interact with each other and the world around us. These technologies have the potential to enhance our relationships by providing us with more personalized and efficient ways to connect. For example, AI-powered virtual assistants could help us manage our busy schedules and keep track of important dates and events. The IoT could connect us to our family and friends through smart homes and wearables, allowing us to communicate with each other seamlessly and easily.

Moreover, emerging technologies such as augmented reality (AR) and virtual reality (VR) are paving the way for new forms of connection. These technologies have the potential to create immersive and engaging environments that can bring people together in new and exciting ways. For example, VR could allow us to attend social events and gatherings from the comfort of our own homes, or even connect us with people from around the world in virtual spaces.

However, as we continue to explore the possibilities of these new technologies, it is important to remember that genuine connection ultimately comes from human interaction and meaningful relationships. While technology can enhance and facilitate these relationships, it cannot replace them entirely. As we move towards a more connected future, it is essential that we find a balance between technology and human interaction, and continue to prioritize the value of genuine connection and relationships.

4.12 Conclusion: Strengthening Our Connections in a Digital World

In conclusion, the rise of digital technology has undoubtedly changed the way we connect with others, but it has not changed the fundamental need for meaningful relationships. If anything, it has highlighted the importance of human connection in an increasingly disconnected world. As we have seen in this chapter, the science of connection is complex and multifaceted. It involves everything from our genes and biology to our social environment and cultural background. However, the key takeaway is that connection is something that can be cultivated and strengthened over time, whether in person or online.

To build genuine connections in a world of digital distractions, we need to be intentional about our relationships. This means taking the time to understand ourselves and others, being present and attentive when we interact, and prioritizing quality over quantity. We also need to be mindful of the risks and downsides of digital technology, such as social media addiction and cyberbullying, and take steps to mitigate these issues.

Ultimately, the algorithmic friend is someone who uses technology to enhance, not replace, their real-life relationships. By using digital tools in a thoughtful and intentional way, we can create more opportunities for connection and deepen our existing relationships. In doing so, we can strengthen our connections in a digital world and lead happier, more fulfilling lives.

5. The Algorithmic Friend: How Technology Can Enhance Our Relationships

5.1 The Benefits of Technology in Relationship Building

The rise of technology has changed the way people interact and build relationships. While some may argue that technology hinders genuine connections, it is undeniable that it also brings benefits to relationship building. Technology has made communication and staying in touch easier and more accessible than ever before. Social media platforms such as Facebook, Instagram, and Twitter have made it possible to connect with friends and family members who are far away, keeping relationships alive despite distance. Additionally, technology has allowed for more efficient and effective communication through messaging apps, video chats, and emails. This has made it easier for individuals to stay connected and maintain relationships, even with busy schedules.

Moreover, technology has also made it possible for individuals to meet new people and broaden their social circle. Dating apps and social networking sites have allowed individuals to find potential partners and new friends with similar interests, allowing them to expand their social network and build new relationships. Additionally, technology has made it easier for individuals to share their experiences and interests with others, enabling people to connect with others who share common interests and passions.

In conclusion, while technology may have its drawbacks, the benefits it brings to relationship building cannot be ignored. With technology, communication has become more accessible, relationships can be maintained despite distance, and individuals can even expand their social circle. As long as technology is used in conjunction with genuine effort and intentionality, it can enhance our relationships and help us build genuine connections in a world of digital distractions.

5.2 The Risks of Over-Reliance on Technology in Relationships

The advances in technology have had a significant impact on the way we interact with one another. It has made communication easier and more accessible, connecting us across vast distances. However, over-reliance on technology in relationships can lead to several risks. The first risk is the loss of intimacy. When we communicate solely through technology, we miss out on the nonverbal cues that are vital for building intimacy. The second risk is the loss of empathy. We tend to be more distant and less empathetic in our online interactions. This can lead to misunderstandings and conflict in our relationships. The third risk is the loss of spontaneity. Technology can make us feel like we have to plan every conversation and interaction, taking the natural flow out of our relationships. The fourth risk is the loss of trust. When we are in a relationship, we tend to rely on our intuition to understand our partner's emotions and needs. However, technology can lead to over-analyzing and misinterpretation of messages, which can create distrust between partners.

To overcome these risks, it is essential to find the right balance between technology and face-to-face interactions in our relationships. We should try to use technology as a tool to enhance our relationships rather than relying on it entirely. It is also crucial to be mindful of the limitations of technology and to recognize when it is best to have a conversation in person. By being intentional and present in our relationships, we can overcome the risks of over-reliance on technology and build deeper, more meaningful connections.

5.3 The Power of Social Media in Connecting People

The power of social media in connecting people cannot be overstated. Social media platforms have revolutionized the way we communicate with each other, enabling us to connect with people from all corners of the world. With just a few clicks, we can reach out to friends, family, and even strangers with whom we share common interests.

One of the most significant benefits of social media is its ability to bring people together. Whether it's through groups, pages, or hashtags, social media has created a virtual space where people can bond over shared passions and interests. This has led to the emergence of online communities that provide a sense of belonging and support to individuals who may feel isolated or marginalized in their real-life environments.

Additionally, social media has made it easier to maintain relationships with people we may not see regularly. With platforms like Facebook and Instagram, we can keep up with the important events in our loved ones' lives, such as birthdays, weddings, and graduations. We can also share our own experiences and updates, allowing others to stay informed about what's going on in our lives.

Social media has also facilitated the formation of new relationships. Dating apps like Tinder and Bumble have made it easier for people to connect with potential partners, while networking platforms like LinkedIn have enabled professionals to expand their networks and find new job opportunities.

Overall, social media has had a profound impact on the way we connect with each other. While it has its downsides, such as the potential for cyberbullying and addiction, its benefits cannot be denied. As we continue to navigate the digital landscape, it's important that we learn to harness the power of social media to build genuine and meaningful connections with others.

5.4 Using Technology to Maintain Long-Distance Relationships

Long-distance relationships can be challenging, especially when it comes to maintaining communication and intimacy. However, with the help of technology, it is now easier than ever to keep in touch with loved ones who are far away. Video calling platforms such as Skype and Zoom, messaging apps like WhatsApp and Facebook Messenger, and social media platforms like Instagram and Facebook allow individuals to stay connected with their partners, friends, and family members regardless of distance.

Using technology to maintain long-distance relationships can also help couples and friends to overcome time differences and busy schedules. With the ability to send instant messages, share photos and videos, and even watch movies or listen to music together online, individuals can stay connected on a regular basis and feel closer to their loved ones.

Technology also offers a range of tools that can help couples and friends to strengthen their relationships. For example, apps like Couple, Happy Couple, and Between are specifically designed to help couples stay connected, share memories, and even plan dates together. Other apps like Avocado and Gaze offer similar features for friends who want to stay in touch and share experiences.

However, it is important to remember that technology should not replace genuine human connection. While it can help to maintain long-distance relationships, it is important to make time for face-to-face interactions whenever possible. By using technology as a tool to enhance our relationships rather than as a substitute for them, we can build stronger, more meaningful connections with the people we care about, regardless of distance.

5.5 Virtual Reality and the Future of Relationship Building

Virtual Reality (VR) has emerged as a powerful tool for enhancing our social interactions, and its potential for relationship building is enormous. Virtual environments enable us to engage with others in a way that is interactive, immersive, and highly engaging. As a result, VR offers an opportunity to create an entirely new kind of social experience, one that transcends the limitations of physical proximity and allows us to connect with people from all over the world in a more meaningful way.

The potential of VR for relationship building is especially significant in the context of long-distance relationships. For many people, maintaining close relationships with loved ones who live far away can be a real challenge. The distance can create a sense of isolation and disconnect, and traditional modes of communication like phone calls, email, and messaging can feel impersonal and unsatisfying. Virtual reality offers a solution to this problem by allowing people to share experiences in real-time, even if they are on opposite sides of the globe.

Moreover, VR can also facilitate the development of new relationships. For example, it could be used to create virtual environments where people can meet, interact, and form social connections based on shared interests and common goals. By removing the barriers of distance and physical space, VR could unlock new opportunities for people to connect with others who share their values and passions, regardless of where they live.

In conclusion, virtual reality has the potential to revolutionize the way we build and maintain relationships, and it is an exciting area of development that should be closely watched. As we continue to explore the possibilities of VR, we may find that it unlocks new opportunities for building genuine connections and creating meaningful relationships with people all over the world.

5.6 Balancing Online and Offline Interactions

In today's world, technology has become an integral part of our daily lives, and it has significantly impacted the way we interact with people. While online interactions have made communication easy and convenient, it has also reduced the need for face-to-face interactions. However, it is crucial to balance both online and offline interactions to maintain healthy relationships. Online interactions can be useful to keep in touch with people who are far away or busy, but it cannot replace face-to-face conversations. We need to make time for offline interactions to strengthen our relationships and build genuine connections.

Balancing online and offline interactions require a conscious effort. We need to set boundaries and limit our online time to make time for offline interactions. When we meet people face-to-face, we can engage in activities that build rapport and create memories, such as having dinner together, going for a walk or doing something fun. These experiences help to create a deeper connection and enhance our relationships.

Moreover, we need to be mindful of our online behaviors and ensure that they reflect our offline personalities. Online interactions can often be misconstrued, and it can be challenging to convey emotions and intentions accurately. Therefore, we need to be mindful of our language, tone, and behaviors while communicating online.

In conclusion, balancing online and offline interactions is crucial to building genuine connections and maintaining healthy relationships. While online interactions can be useful, it cannot replace face-to-face conversations, and we need to make time for offline interactions to create deeper connections. By being mindful of our online behaviors and setting boundaries, we can strike a balance between online and offline interactions and build meaningful relationships.

5.7 The Importance of Intentionality in Using Technology to Connect with Others

Technology has revolutionized the way we communicate and connect with others. With just a few taps on a screen, we can instantly reach friends and family members from all over the world. However, in the midst of our digital age, it's easy to forget the importance of intentionality when using technology to connect with others. It's not enough to simply send a message or a friend request and assume that we've done our part to maintain a relationship. Instead, we must be intentional in our actions and use technology to enhance, not replace, genuine connections.

One of the key ways we can be intentional is by being present in our interactions with others. This means putting away distractions and giving our full attention to the person we're communicating with. It also means taking the time to craft thoughtful messages and responses, rather than simply sending off a generic "Hey, how are you?" We must also be mindful of our tone and language, as technology can often obscure our true intentions and emotions.

Another way to be intentional is by using technology to facilitate deeper, more meaningful conversations. This can include video calls, voice messages, or even sharing articles or podcasts that we think the other person would find interesting. By taking the time to engage in thoughtful conversations and share meaningful content, we can build stronger connections with those we care about.

In short, the key to using technology to connect with others is intentionality. By being present, mindful, and thoughtful in our interactions, we can use technology to enhance our relationships and build genuine connections in a world of digital distractions.

5.8 Building Trust in Digital Relationships

Building trust in digital relationships is crucial to forming genuine connections in a world of digital distractions. In traditional face-to-face interactions, trust can be established through body language, tone of voice, and other nonverbal cues. In a digital context, nonverbal communication is largely absent, making trust-building more challenging. One way to build trust in digital relationships is through consistent and authentic communication. This means being transparent about intentions and consistently following through on promises. Another important aspect of building trust in digital relationships is maintaining confidentiality and privacy. People need to feel confident that their personal information will be protected when interacting with others online. In addition, it is essential to be respectful and considerate in online interactions, as this can convey a sense of empathy and understanding. Finally, it is important to acknowledge and take responsibility when mistakes are made, as this can demonstrate honesty and accountability. Building trust in digital relationships requires effort and intentionality, but the rewards are worth it. When trust is established, individuals are more likely to feel comfortable sharing their thoughts and feelings, leading to deeper and more meaningful connections. Overall, by prioritizing transparency, confidentiality, respect, and responsibility, individuals can build trust in their digital relationships and cultivate genuine connections in a world that is increasingly driven by technology.

5.9 Using Technology to Enhance In-Person Connections

Technology has become an integral part of our daily lives, and it is now an essential tool that we use to foster personal connections. In today's world, where people are constantly distracted by technology, it can be challenging to establish genuine connections with others. However, technology can also be used as a tool to enhance our in-person connections. For example, social media platforms provide a means to stay connected with friends and family, even if they are far away. Additionally, video conferencing has become a popular way for people to maintain personal and professional relationships.

Moreover, technology can also be used to facilitate meaningful conversations between people. There are several applications that are designed specifically for this purpose, such as Icebreaker and We3. Such applications use advanced algorithms to match like-minded individuals who may not have had the opportunity to meet otherwise. This technology can be particularly helpful for people who struggle to make connections in social settings.

Technology can also be used to enhance in-person meetings and events. For example, event management software can be used to streamline the planning and organization of events. Additionally, interactive displays and digital signage can be used to enhance the attendee experience, providing information and entertainment to those in attendance.

In conclusion, technology can be a powerful tool that we can use to enhance our personal connections. It provides us with the means to stay connected with friends and family, facilitates meaningful conversations, and enhances in-person meetings and events. By utilizing technology effectively, we can build more genuine connections in a world that is becoming increasingly digital.

5.10 The Ethics of Algorithmic Friendship

The rise of technology has brought significant changes in the way people interact with each other. Nowadays, friendships can be formed and maintained through digital platforms such as social media sites, messaging apps, and online communities. These algorithmic friendships offer various benefits, including convenience, the ability to connect with people from different parts of the world, and access to a vast pool of information.

However, as with any technological development, algorithmic friendships raise ethical concerns. One issue is the potential for these friendships to be superficial and lacking in genuine emotional connection. Due to the nature of digital communications, it can be challenging to build deep, meaningful relationships with people solely through online interactions. As such, algorithmic friendships may be more prone to a lack of authenticity, leading to a sense of loneliness and disconnection.

Another ethical concern is the possibility of algorithmic friendships being used to manipulate or exploit people. Companies and individuals can use the vast amounts of data gathered through these digital platforms to target individuals with specific content or products. This can be done without the user's knowledge or consent, potentially leading to issues with privacy and informed consent.

Moreover, algorithmic friendships can also perpetuate social inequality, as the algorithms used to connect people may be biased towards certain demographics based on location, interests, and other factors. This can result in a lack of diversity in the people one interacts with, leading to a limited worldview and reinforcing existing prejudices and biases.

In conclusion, while algorithmic friendships offer several benefits, it is essential to consider the ethical implications of these relationships. It is crucial to build genuine connections, ensure informed consent, and avoid perpetuating existing inequalities to make technology a force for good in building meaningful relationships.

5.11 Conclusion: Leveraging Technology to Build More Meaningful Relationships

In conclusion, technology has drastically changed the way we interact and build relationships with others. While some argue that technology hinders our ability to form genuine connections, it has also opened up new opportunities for us to connect with people from all over the world. Platforms like social media have allowed us to maintain relationships with people we may have lost touch with otherwise, while dating apps have made it easier for people to find compatible partners. However, it is important to recognize that technology should not replace face-to-face interactions and genuine connections. We must remember that behind every screen is a real human being with their own thoughts, feelings, and experiences. It is important to use technology as a tool to enhance our relationships rather than a replacement for them. As we continue to navigate the ever-evolving landscape of technology, it is vital that we prioritize building meaningful relationships and fostering genuine connections. By leveraging technology in meaningful ways, we can strengthen our relationships and create a more connected world. Ultimately, it is up to us to use technology in a way that serves us rather than hinders us, and to constantly seek out new ways to build genuine connections in a world of digital distractions.

6. Creating Boundaries: Balancing Technology Use and Real-Life Connections

6.1 The Importance of Setting Boundaries

Setting boundaries is essential to maintaining healthy relationships and establishing our priorities. In the age of digital distractions, boundaries are more important than ever. With social media, email, messaging apps, and other technological tools at our fingertips, it can be easy to let our digital lives consume our real-life connections. However, by taking the time to set boundaries, we can ensure that our relationships remain meaningful and fulfilling.

One of the most important aspects of setting boundaries is understanding what our priorities are. We need to determine what is important to us and make sure that our time and energy are being directed towards those things. This might mean limiting the amount of time we spend on social media, turning off notifications during certain times of the day, or setting rules about when and where we use our devices.

Another important aspect of setting boundaries is being clear about our expectations. We need to communicate with the people in our lives about what we are and are not comfortable with when it comes to technology use. This might mean asking friends and family members to refrain from using their phones during meal times, or letting coworkers know that we will not be responding to emails after a certain hour.

Ultimately, setting boundaries is about taking control of our digital lives and using technology in a way that supports our real-life connections. By being intentional about how we use technology, we can create a healthier and more fulfilling life for ourselves and those around us.

6.2 Understanding Your Unique Boundaries

is crucial in maintaining a healthy balance between the use of technology and real-life connections. Every individual has their own set of beliefs, values, and priorities that have a significant impact on their relationship with technology. For instance, some people might use social media to stay connected with friends and family, while others prefer to limit their exposure. Similarly, some individuals might enjoy spending time playing video games, while some might find it unproductive.

It is vital to identify and set boundaries that align with your values, beliefs, and priorities. This requires self-awareness and an understanding of the impact of technology on your life. You need to ask yourself questions such as: What role does technology play in my life? How does it impact my relationships, productivity, and mental health? What am I comfortable sharing online, and with whom?

Once you have identified your boundaries, it is essential to communicate them effectively with your friends, family, and colleagues. This can help avoid misunderstandings and conflicts arising from mismatched expectations. For instance, if you have decided to limit your social media use, you can inform your friends and family about it, so they don't feel ignored or neglected.

In conclusion, creating boundaries is a personal journey that requires self-reflection and self-awareness. It is important to remember that your boundaries might be different from others, and that's okay. The key is to identify and communicate them effectively to maintain healthy relationships with technology and real-life connections.

6.3 Communicating Your Boundaries to Others

Communicating your boundaries to others is a vital aspect of creating healthy relationships in the digital age. It is important to be clear about what you are comfortable with and what you are not comfortable with, and to communicate that to the people in your life. This could include things like not responding to work emails after a certain time, not checking your phone during meals, or not engaging in certain kinds of social media interactions. It is important to remember that setting boundaries is not about being selfish or demanding, but rather, it is about taking care of yourself and your well-being.

When communicating your boundaries to others, it is important to do so in a clear and respectful manner. Start by identifying the specific boundary you want to establish and why it is important to you. Then, communicate that boundary to the other person in a calm and respectful way. Be prepared to listen to their response and to negotiate if necessary, but ultimately, be firm in your boundaries.

It is also important to remember that boundaries are not set in stone, and they may need to be adjusted over time. As your life and circumstances change, your boundaries may need to change as well. It is important to be flexible and willing to adapt as needed.

Communicating your boundaries to others can be challenging, but it is an important step in building genuine connections in a world of digital distractions. By being clear and respectful about your needs and limits, you can create healthier and more fulfilling relationships with the people in your life.

6.4 Creating a Healthy Relationship with Technology

Creating a healthy relationship with technology is important for maintaining a balanced lifestyle. It is easy to become consumed by technology and forget about the importance of face-to-face interactions and real-life connections. In order to create a healthy relationship with technology, it is important to establish boundaries and limit the amount of time spent on devices.

One way to create boundaries is to set specific times for technology use. For example, only allowing the use of technology during designated hours of the day or for a specific amount of time. This can help prevent technology from taking over and allow for time to engage in other activities.

Another important aspect of creating a healthy relationship with technology is to be mindful of the impact it has on mental health. Social media and constant connectivity can lead to feelings of anxiety and stress. It is important to take breaks from technology and engage in activities that promote relaxation and well-being, such as exercise, meditation, or spending time in nature.

It is also important to prioritize in-person connections and relationships. Technology can be a useful tool for staying in touch, but it should not replace face-to-face interactions. Making an effort to spend time with friends and family in person can help strengthen relationships and prevent feelings of isolation.

In conclusion, creating a healthy relationship with technology requires establishing boundaries, being mindful of its impact on mental health, and prioritizing in-person connections. By finding a balance between technology use and real-life interactions, individuals can lead a more fulfilling and well-rounded life.

6.5 Balancing Screen Time with Real-Life Connections

In today's digitally driven world, it can be challenging to balance screen time with real-life connections. It's easy to get lost in the constant stream of notifications, updates, and news feeds. However, it's essential to prioritize genuine connections with people in the real world. Technology has revolutionized the way we communicate, making it easier than ever to stay connected with friends, family, and colleagues. But relying solely on digital communication can be detrimental to our mental and emotional well-being. It's crucial to set healthy boundaries and find a balance between technology and real-life connections.

One way to balance screen time with real-life connections is to set aside specific times of the day for tech-free activities. This could be anything from going for a walk in the park to having a coffee with a friend. It's also essential to be present in the moment and give people our undivided attention when we're with them. Put your phone away, turn off notifications, and be fully engaged in the conversation. This shows that you value the connection and respect the person's time.

Another way to balance screen time is to limit the use of technology during certain times of the day, such as meal times or before bedtime. This not only helps to reduce screen time but also improves sleep quality and overall well-being. It's also important to remember that while technology can enhance our connections with people, it shouldn't replace them entirely. Genuine connections are built on shared experiences and real-life interactions. Therefore, it's essential to make time for face-to-face interactions and cultivate meaningful relationships with people in the real world.

6.6 Learning to Say No to Distractions

Learning to say no to distractions is essential if we want to build genuine connections in a world of digital distractions. With an abundance of technology at our fingertips, it's easy to get caught up in the never-ending stream of notifications, messages, and alerts. However, constantly being connected to our devices can have detrimental effects on our ability to connect with others and be present in the moment.

To say no to distractions, we need to establish boundaries and prioritize our time. This means setting aside specific times for technology use and limiting our exposure to it during certain hours of the day. Additionally, we need to be mindful of the type of technology we are using and how it can impact our relationships. For instance, social media can be a great tool for staying in touch with friends and family, but it can also be a major time-waster and distract us from meaningful interactions.

Another way to say no to distractions is to practice mindfulness and be present in the moment. This means focusing on the person or task in front of us and avoiding the temptation to check our phones or get sidetracked by other digital distractions. By being fully present, we can deepen our connections with others and improve our overall well-being.

It's important to remember that saying no to distractions doesn't mean we have to completely disconnect from technology. Rather, it means finding a healthy balance between digital and real-life connections and prioritizing our time accordingly. By doing so, we can build more meaningful relationships and live a more fulfilling life.

6.7 Avoiding Burnout: The Benefits of Unplugging

In today's digital age, it's easy to get consumed by technology and the constant notifications that come with it. Many of us feel the pressure to always be connected, but this can often lead to burnout. It's important to recognize the benefits of unplugging and disconnecting from technology from time to time. By doing so, we allow ourselves to recharge and focus on our real-life connections.

Unplugging can be as simple as turning off your phone for a few hours or leaving it at home when you go out for a walk or a meal with friends. When we disconnect from technology, we give ourselves the opportunity to be present in the moment and fully engage with those around us. We can focus on our own thoughts and feelings, rather than constantly being distracted by notifications and updates.

In addition to improving our real-life connections, unplugging can also have other benefits for our mental health. Research has shown that excessive technology use can lead to feelings of anxiety and depression. By taking breaks from technology, we can reduce these negative effects and improve our overall well-being.

Ultimately, the benefits of unplugging are numerous. By taking time to disconnect from technology, we can improve our real-life connections and our mental health. So, next time you feel overwhelmed by technology, try unplugging and see how it can improve your life.

6.8 Prioritizing Face-to-Face Interactions

In today's world of constant connectivity, it can be easy to get lost in the endless stream of digital interactions. However, it is important to prioritize face-to-face interactions to build genuine connections with others. While technology can facilitate communication, it lacks the emotional depth and nuance that comes from in-person conversations. It is important to set aside time to meet with friends, family, and colleagues in person to strengthen relationships and create lasting memories.

In a world where social media and messaging apps are prevalent, face-to-face interactions offer a chance to truly connect with others. Body language, tone of voice, and facial expressions all play a role in how we communicate and understand one another. These nonverbal cues cannot be fully conveyed through text or messaging, which can lead to misunderstandings and miscommunications. Meeting in person allows for a deeper connection and a greater understanding of the other person's thoughts and feelings.

In addition, face-to-face interactions offer a break from the constant stimulation of technology. It allows us to be present in the moment and fully engage with those around us. By prioritizing face-to-face interactions, we are able to create meaningful connections and a sense of community.

In conclusion, while technology can be helpful in facilitating communication, it cannot replace the emotional depth and connection that comes from in-person interactions. By prioritizing face-to-face interactions, we are able to build genuine relationships and create lasting memories. It is important to set aside time for these interactions to strengthen connections and create a sense of community in our increasingly digital world.

6.9 Redefining Productivity: Quality Connections over Quantity of Work

The traditional definition of productivity has often been associated with the amount of work an individual can complete in a given timeframe. However, this notion is quickly becoming outdated as technology continues to dominate our lives. In today's fast-paced digital world, the focus is shifting from quantity to quality, and the emphasis is on building genuine connections rather than just completing tasks. Redefining productivity means prioritizing meaningful interactions over mindless work. It's about finding the right balance between technology use and real-life connections.

In the age of social media, the concept of connection has been reduced to a mere number of followers or likes. However, true connections go much deeper than these superficial metrics. Quality connections involve actively engaging with others and building meaningful relationships based on shared values and interests. It's about being present in the moment and truly listening to others rather than just scrolling through our newsfeed.

To achieve this, we need to set boundaries around our technology use and prioritize real-life interactions. It's about being intentional with our time and energy and focusing on activities that nourish our relationships rather than just filling up our schedules. This can be as simple as scheduling regular face-to-face meetings with friends or family or setting aside dedicated time for phone or video calls.

Ultimately, redefining productivity means embracing a more holistic approach to life that values quality over quantity. It's about breaking free from the constant distractions of technology and focusing on what really matters: building genuine connections with the people around us. By doing so, we can create more meaningful and fulfilling lives that are grounded in true human connection.

6.10 Building a Supportive Community for Boundaries and Connection.

Building a supportive community for boundaries and connection is crucial to maintaining a healthy balance between technology use and real-life connections. This community can be made up of friends, family, colleagues, or even strangers who share similar values and goals. The first step in building this community is to be open and honest about your boundaries and the reasons behind them. This can help others understand your perspective and support your choices. It is also important to listen to others' boundaries and respect their choices, even if they differ from your own.

Another way to build a supportive community is to find groups or organizations that align with your values and interests. This can include social clubs, volunteer groups, or online communities. These groups can provide a sense of belonging, support, and accountability as you work towards your goals.

In addition, it is important to prioritize real-life connections and create opportunities for face-to-face interactions. This can include scheduling regular social events, attending community gatherings, or simply making time for one-on-one conversations with friends and family.

Ultimately, building a supportive community for boundaries and connection requires effort and intentionality. It may involve stepping out of your comfort zone and being vulnerable, but the rewards of stronger relationships and a healthier relationship with technology make it worth the effort.

7. Authentic Communication: Tips for Building Meaningful Conversations Online and Offline

7.1 The Importance of Active Listening

The importance of active listening cannot be overstated in the realm of authentic communication. Active listening is the foundation of building meaningful connections with others, both online and offline. It involves fully engaging with the speaker, giving them your undivided attention, and demonstrating empathy and understanding.

Effective communication is not just about speaking and expressing oneself, but also about being receptive to others' perspectives and experiences. Active listening is a crucial component of receptive communication, as it allows us to hear and process information accurately and thoroughly. By actively listening to others, we can gain a deeper understanding of their thoughts, feelings, and needs, which in turn helps us build stronger, more meaningful relationships.

In the digital age, where distractions abound and people are more connected than ever before, active listening has become all the more important. With the constant barrage of notifications, messages, and alerts, it can be easy to become distracted and disengaged from conversations. However, by consciously choosing to practice active listening, we can counteract these distractions and build more authentic connections with others.

Active listening requires patience, focus, and an open mind. It involves setting aside one's own biases and assumptions in order to truly hear and understand the speaker. It may take practice and effort to develop active listening skills, but the rewards are well worth it. By learning to listen actively, we can build more fulfilling relationships, deepen our understanding of others, and ultimately, cultivate a more empathetic and compassionate society.

7.2 Asking Open-Ended Questions

Asking open-ended questions is a crucial skill when it comes to building meaningful conversations online and offline. Open-ended questions are designed to elicit more than just a one-word answer, in comparison to closed-ended questions that can only be answered with a yes or no response. These questions encourage the speaker to share their thoughts, feelings, and opinions, leading to a deeper level of engagement and connection. When we ask open-ended questions, we show that we are genuinely interested in the other person's perspective and we give them the space to express themselves fully.

Asking open-ended questions can be especially helpful in online communication, where it can be more challenging to convey tone and intention. By asking thoughtful questions, we can show that we are actively listening and engaging with the conversation, even if we are not physically present. Additionally, open-ended questions can help us navigate difficult topics and navigate disagreements or misunderstandings. When we approach these situations with curiosity and a willingness to learn, we create an environment of trust and respect that can ultimately strengthen our relationships.

To be effective at asking open-ended questions, it's important to be intentional and thoughtful in our approach. We should avoid leading questions that suggest a particular answer or judgment, and instead, focus on questions that invite the other person to share their own experience. Additionally, we should be prepared to listen actively and respond empathetically, creating a safe and supportive space for the other person to share. By incorporating open-ended questions into our conversations, we can build stronger, more meaningful connections with those around us.

7.3 Practicing Mindful Communication

Practicing mindful communication is essential to building meaningful connections both online and offline. Mindful communication involves being present in the moment, listening actively, and responding with intention. In our fast-paced digital world, it can be easy to fall into the trap of multitasking or constantly checking our phones while in conversation with others. However, this behavior can be detrimental to our relationships and our ability to connect authentically with others.

To practice mindful communication, it is important to set aside distractions and give our full attention to the person we are speaking with. This means making eye contact, actively listening to what they are saying, and responding thoughtfully. It also means being aware of our own thoughts and feelings and how they may be impacting our communication.

In addition to being present in the moment, practicing mindful communication also involves being aware of our tone and body language. Our nonverbal cues can communicate just as much as our words, so it is important to be mindful of how we are coming across to others.

Overall, practicing mindful communication requires us to slow down and be intentional in our interactions with others. By doing so, we can develop deeper connections and build relationships based on authenticity and mutual understanding.

7.4 Building Trust Through Vulnerability

In a world where social media and digital communication are the norm, building trust can be a daunting task. However, one effective way to establish a connection with someone is by being vulnerable. Vulnerability may seem counterintuitive, as it involves opening oneself up to the possibility of being hurt or rejected. But, when done in a safe and appropriate setting, vulnerability can help create a sense of empathy and mutual understanding.

Sharing personal experiences and feelings can also help others feel more comfortable opening up, creating a positive feedback loop of trust and authenticity. It's important to note that vulnerability does not mean oversharing or revealing too much too soon. Trust is built gradually, and it's important to be aware of boundaries and respect the other person's comfort level.

Vulnerability can also help break down barriers and dispel preconceived notions about a person or group. By sharing personal experiences, one can challenge stereotypes or assumptions that others may have. This can create a space for open dialogue and help build bridges between people with different backgrounds or experiences.

In short, vulnerability can be a powerful tool in building trust and fostering genuine connections. It requires courage and a willingness to be open and honest, but the rewards can be significant. By creating an environment of trust and authenticity, we can build stronger relationships both online and offline.

7.5 The Power of Empathy in Communication

Empathy is the ability to understand and share the feelings of others. It is a powerful tool in communication because it allows us to connect with others on a deeper level. When we show empathy, we are showing that we care about the other person's feelings and that we are willing to listen and understand their point of view. This is especially important in today's world where communication often takes place online, where it can be easy to misinterpret tone and intention. By showing empathy, we can build trust and create meaningful connections with others, even in the digital world.

One of the keys to showing empathy is active listening. This means giving the other person our full attention and really trying to understand what they are saying. It also means paying attention to nonverbal cues like body language and tone of voice. When we actively listen, we are showing the other person that we respect and value their thoughts and feelings.

Another important aspect of empathy is perspective-taking. This means putting ourselves in the other person's shoes and trying to understand things from their point of view. This can be especially challenging when we disagree with someone, but it is important to remember that everyone has their own experiences and beliefs that shape their perspective.

Showing empathy in communication can be difficult, but the rewards are worth it. By building meaningful connections with others, we can create a sense of belonging and fulfillment in our lives. So next time you are communicating with someone, try to put yourself in their shoes and really listen to what they have to say. You may be surprised at how much more meaningful your conversations become.

7.6 Overcoming Communication Barriers

In today's world, communication barriers are a common problem that people face. These barriers can arise from various factors such as cultural differences, language barriers, technological challenges, and even personal biases. In order to build genuine connections with people, it is important to overcome these communication barriers.

One of the most effective ways to overcome communication barriers is to practice active listening. Active listening involves paying attention to what the other person is saying and showing that you understand them by paraphrasing or summarizing their words. This helps to ensure that both parties are on the same page and can avoid misunderstandings.

Another way to overcome communication barriers is to be aware of cultural differences. It is important to understand and respect different cultural norms and practices. This can involve things like being aware of nonverbal cues or avoiding certain topics of conversation that might be considered taboo in a particular culture.

Using technology to our advantage can also help to overcome communication barriers. For example, video conferencing can be used to facilitate communication with people who are far away or who speak different languages. There are also translation apps available that can help in overcoming language barriers.

Finally, it is important to be aware of our own biases and to actively work to overcome them. This can involve things like seeking out diverse perspectives and challenging our own assumptions.

By being proactive and taking steps to overcome communication barriers, we can build more meaningful and genuine connections with others. This is an important part of building relationships in today's digital world.

7.7 The Art of Small Talk

The art of small talk is often underestimated and undervalued, but it is a crucial component of building meaningful connections with others. Small talk is not just idle chatter or a way to pass the time; it is a way to establish a rapport with someone, to show that you are interested in them, and to create the foundation for deeper conversations in the future. To be skilled at small talk, it is important to be able to read social cues and understand the context of the conversation. This means knowing when to ask open-ended questions, when to share a personal anecdote, and when to listen attentively. It also means being able to adapt to different settings and the people you are speaking with, whether you are at a networking event, a social gathering, or just chatting with someone in line at the grocery store.

One of the keys to successful small talk is to find common ground with the person you are speaking with. This can be anything from the weather to a shared interest or experience. It is also important to be genuine and authentic in your interactions, avoiding scripted or rehearsed responses. Remember that small talk is just the beginning of a conversation and that it can lead to deeper and more meaningful connections if approached with an open mind and a willingness to engage. In a world of digital distractions, the art of small talk can be a powerful tool for building genuine connections with others, both online and offline. By taking the time to engage in authentic conversations with those around us, we can break down barriers and create a more connected and compassionate world.

7.8 Creating Meaningful Conversations Online

Creating meaningful conversations online can be challenging, but it's not impossible. The key is to approach each conversation with intention and authenticity. Before engaging in a conversation, ask yourself what you hope to gain from it. Are you looking to learn something new, share your own experiences, or simply connect with someone else? Once you know your objective, it's easier to guide the conversation in a direction that is meaningful for both parties.

One of the most important elements of meaningful conversations is active listening. When you're engaged in an online conversation, it's easy to get distracted by other notifications or tasks. However, giving your full attention to the person you're speaking with demonstrates that you value their thoughts and opinions. Ask open-ended questions to encourage the other person to share more about their experiences and perspectives.

Another way to create meaningful conversations online is to share your own vulnerability. This might mean admitting your own struggles or insecurities, or simply expressing your emotions authentically. When you share your genuine feelings, you create a safe space for the other person to do the same.

Finally, remember that meaningful conversations can happen in any format. Whether you're sending a message, commenting on a post, or having a video chat, what matters most is the quality of the interaction. Be present, listen actively, and express yourself honestly to build genuine connections online.

7.9 Tips for Avoiding Misunderstandings in Digital Communication

Digital communication has become an integral part of our lives, and it is essential to know how to avoid misunderstandings to have meaningful conversations. Here are some tips to follow:

1. Be clear and concise: When communicating online, it is crucial to be clear and concise. Avoid using ambiguous terms or phrases that can be interpreted in multiple ways. Use simple and straightforward language that everyone can understand.

2. Use emoticons: Emoticons can help add context to your message and convey your emotions effectively. They can also help to soften a message that may come across as too direct.

3. Be aware of cultural differences: Different cultures have different ways of communicating, and it is essential to be aware of these

differences. For example, in some cultures, direct communication is considered rude, while in others, it's the norm.

4. Avoid using all caps: Writing in all caps can come across as shouting, so avoid using them unless you want to emphasize something.

5. Read your message before sending it: Before sending a message, take a moment to read it back to yourself. This can help you spot any mistakes or misunderstandings before they happen.

6. Take a break if you're feeling emotional: If you're feeling emotional, it's best to take a break before responding to a message. This can help you to calm down and avoid saying something you may regret later.

By following these tips, you can avoid misunderstandings and have more authentic and meaningful conversations online.

7.10 Using Social Media to Connect Authentically

Social media has become an integral part of our lives, allowing us to connect with people from all over the world. However, the downside of social media is that it can often feel superficial, with people presenting curated versions of themselves and their lives. To connect authentically on social media, it's important to be genuine and vulnerable. Social media is a great platform to share your thoughts and feelings, but it's important to remember that not everything needs to be shared publicly. Be selective about what you share and make sure it aligns with your values and beliefs.

Another way to connect authentically on social media is to engage with others in meaningful conversations. Avoid small talk and instead ask open-ended questions that encourage deeper conversations. Listen actively and respond thoughtfully, showing genuine interest in what the other person has to say. It's also important to be respectful and considerate, especially when discussing sensitive topics.

In addition to engaging with others, it's important to be authentic in how you present yourself on social media. Don't feel pressured to present a perfect image of yourself, as this can be exhausting and unattainable. Instead, be honest about your strengths and weaknesses, and share your unique perspectives. This will help you connect with like-minded individuals, and build genuine connections that go beyond surface-level interactions.

Overall, social media can be a powerful tool for connecting with others authentically, but it requires intentionality and mindfulness. By being genuine, engaging with others thoughtfully, and presenting yourself authentically, you can build meaningful relationships that enrich your life both online and offline.

7.11 Nurturing Relationships with Remote Communication

In today's world, remote communication has become an integral part of our lives. With the ongoing pandemic, it has become even more important to nurture relationships through online channels. The key to building meaningful connections through remote communication lies in authenticity and genuineness. It is crucial to communicate with an open mind and listen to the other person attentively, whether it is through video calls or messaging platforms.

Moreover, it is important to make an effort to connect with people on a personal level, regardless of the distance. This can be done by sharing personal experiences, asking about their day, and showing interest in their lives. It is also important to give them the space to express themselves freely and without judgment.

In addition to empathy and listening skills, it is also essential to establish boundaries and respect them. This includes setting specific times for communication and avoiding distractions. It is important to create a conducive environment for communication, free from distractions and interruptions, to ensure that the conversation is meaningful and productive.

Lastly, it is important to be patient and understanding, especially when it comes to cultural differences and language barriers. We must be willing to learn and adapt to different communication styles and preferences, and make an effort to bridge any gaps in understanding.

In summary, nurturing relationships through remote communication requires authenticity, empathy, active listening, respect for boundaries, and patience. These skills are essential in building meaningful connections in a world dominated by digital distractions.

7.12 Building Deeper Connections Through Shared Experiences

Building deeper connections through shared experiences is an absolute essential for building genuine connections in the world of digital distractions. The power of shared experiences is immense and cannot be understated. When we go through something together, it creates a sense of belonging and oneness that is hard to replicate in any other way. Shared experiences also give us a common ground to build upon and can create a foundation for lasting relationships. One of the reasons why we find it difficult to build meaningful connections online is that we are often just communicating with words and emojis, and there is a lack of shared experience. To create deeper connections, we need to move beyond the superficial and have more meaningful conversations that are based on shared experiences.

One effective way to build deeper connections through shared experiences is to participate in activities that involve teamwork and collaboration. When people work together towards a common goal, they form a bond that goes beyond the task at hand. Activities such as group hikes, volunteering, or team-building exercises are great ways to build deeper connections because they require people to work together and share experiences. Another way to build deeper connections is to attend events or gatherings that are based on shared interests. For example, if you are a music lover, attending concerts or festivals can be an excellent way to connect with like-minded people who share your passion.

Building deeper connections through shared experiences requires a willingness to step out of your comfort zone and try new things. It also requires active participation and engagement with others. When we are willing to put ourselves out there, we open ourselves up to the possibility of forming deeper connections with others. By prioritizing shared experiences and seeking out opportunities to connect with others, we can build genuine connections that transcend the digital world.

7.13 The Role of Humor in Communication

Humor plays a crucial role in communication, whether online or offline. It helps create a positive and inviting atmosphere that encourages people to engage in meaningful conversations. Humor can also break down barriers and reduce tension, making it easier for people to connect with one another. When people share a laugh, they are more likely to be open to hearing different perspectives and ideas, which can lead to more productive discussions.

Humor can also be a powerful tool for building rapport and trust. When people share a sense of humor, they feel more connected and comfortable with one another. This can make it easier to build authentic relationships based on mutual respect and understanding.

However, it is important to use humor appropriately and in a way that is respectful to others. Humor that is offensive or insensitive can create a negative atmosphere and damage relationships. It is also important to recognize that not everyone shares the same sense of humor, so it is important to be mindful of this when using humor in communication.

In summary, humor is an important aspect of communication that can help build relationships and facilitate meaningful conversations.

When used appropriately, it can create a positive and inviting atmosphere that encourages people to engage with one another. However, it is important to use humor in a way that is respectful to others and to recognize that not everyone shares the same sense of humor.

7.14 Communicating with Different Personality Types.

Communicating with different personality types can be challenging, but it is an essential skill for building genuine connections. Understanding the different personality types can help you tailor your communication style to meet the needs of the person you are interacting with. There are several personality typing systems, including the Myers-Briggs Type Indicator and the Big Five Personality Traits. These systems can help you identify personality traits such as introversion/extroversion, openness, conscientiousness, agreeableness, and neuroticism.

When communicating with introverted individuals, it is important to give them space and time to process their thoughts before responding. They may prefer written communication over face-to-face interactions. On the other hand, extroverted individuals may thrive in group settings and enjoy brainstorming sessions. They may prefer face-to-face interactions over written communication.

Those who score high in openness tend to enjoy new experiences and ideas. You can appeal to their sense of creativity by presenting new ideas and concepts. Conscientious individuals value structure and organization, so it is important to be clear and concise when communicating with them. Agreeable individuals tend to prioritize harmony and may avoid conflict, so it is essential to approach them with empathy and understanding.

Finally, individuals scoring high in neuroticism may be prone to anxiety and worry. They may need reassurance and support in their communications. By understanding these personality types, you can tailor your communication style to build meaningful connections with others.

8. Cultivating Empathy: Understanding and Respecting Others in a Digital Age

8.1 The Importance of Empathy in a Digital World

In today's fast-paced digital world, it is more important than ever to cultivate empathy. Empathy is the ability to understand and share the feelings of others, and it plays a crucial role in building genuine connections with others. In a world where communication is often digital and lacking in face-to-face interaction, it can be easy to forget the importance of empathy. However, ignoring empathy can have serious consequences for our relationships and our society as a whole.

One of the biggest challenges in cultivating empathy in a digital world is the prevalence of social media and online communication. While these tools can be great for staying connected with others, they can also create a sense of distance and detachment that can hinder empathy. When we communicate with others online, it can be easy to forget that there is a real person on the other end of the conversation. This can lead to a lack of empathy and understanding, which can ultimately damage our relationships.

To combat this, it is important to make a conscious effort to practice empathy in all of our interactions, both online and offline. This means taking the time to truly listen to others, trying to understand their perspective, and showing compassion and understanding. It also means being mindful of our own biases and assumptions, and being open to learning from others.

Ultimately, empathy is essential for building genuine connections and fostering a sense of community in a digital age. By cultivating empathy, we can create a more compassionate and understanding society, one where we can truly connect with each other on a deeper level.

8.2 Overcoming Barriers to Empathy in the Digital Age

The digital age has brought tremendous advancements in technology, communication, and connectivity. However, it has also created barriers to empathy and genuine human connections. One of the biggest barriers is the lack of face-to-face communication, which can hinder the development of empathy by depriving us of important social cues such as body language, tone of voice, and facial expressions. This, in turn, can lead to misinterpretations, misunderstandings, and a lack of emotional connection.

Another barrier is the prevalence of social media and online communication, which can encourage superficial interactions and discourage deeper, more meaningful conversations. Social media can also create an echo chamber effect, where we are exposed only to viewpoints and opinions that align with our own, reinforcing our biases and making it harder to empathize with those who have different perspectives.

To overcome these barriers, we need to be intentional in our communication and actively seek out opportunities for genuine connection. This can involve stepping away from our screens and engaging in face-to-face interactions, or using technology to facilitate deeper conversations and connections. It also means being open to diverse viewpoints and actively seeking out perspectives that challenge our own.

Ultimately, cultivating empathy in the digital age requires a willingness to be vulnerable and to embrace our shared humanity. By recognizing and valuing the experiences and emotions of others, we can build genuine connections that transcend the boundaries of technology and help us to better understand and respect one another.

8.3 Developing Empathy: Tips and Exercises

Developing empathy is an essential skill that everyone should possess. It is the ability to understand and share the feelings of others. Empathy allows us to connect with others on a deeper level, helping us to build relationships and foster a sense of community. In today's digital age, it is more important than ever to cultivate empathy. Social media has made it easy to connect with others, but it can also be a breeding ground for misunderstandings and conflict. Here are some tips and exercises that can help you develop empathy.

Firstly, put yourself in someone else's shoes. When you encounter a situation, try to imagine how it would feel if you were in that person's position. This exercise will help you develop a better understanding of their feelings and motivations.

Secondly, listen actively. When someone is sharing their thoughts and feelings with you, be present in the moment and actively listen to them. Avoid interrupting, judging, or dismissing their feelings. Instead, try to understand their perspective and ask questions to clarify any misunderstandings.

Thirdly, practice kindness. Small acts of kindness can go a long way in developing empathy. Simple gestures like holding the door open for someone, offering a compliment, or lending a helping hand can help create a positive environment and build relationships.

Lastly, seek out diverse perspectives. Engage in conversations with people who have different views and experiences from your own. This will help you broaden your understanding of the world and develop empathy for others.

In conclusion, developing empathy is a lifelong process that requires practice and intentionality. By putting yourself in someone else's shoes, actively listening, practicing kindness, and seeking out diverse perspectives, you can cultivate empathy and build genuine connections in a world of digital distractions.

8.4 The Role of Active Listening in Empathy

The role of active listening in empathy cannot be overstated. Empathy involves understanding and respecting the feelings and experiences of others, and active listening is a key component of achieving this understanding. When we actively listen, we give our full attention to the person speaking, without interrupting or judging them. This allows us to fully absorb their words and emotions, and respond in a way that shows we genuinely care about them.

Active listening involves more than just hearing the words someone is saying. It involves paying attention to their tone of voice, body language, and other nonverbal cues. It also involves asking clarifying questions and reflecting back what we have heard, to ensure we have fully understood the other person's perspective.

In a world of digital distractions, active listening can be a challenge. We are often bombarded with notifications, messages, and other interruptions that can pull us away from the person we are speaking with. However, it is important that we make a conscious effort to be present in our interactions with others, and to give them our full attention.

By practicing active listening, we can build stronger relationships with others, and better understand their needs and perspectives. This can lead to greater empathy and compassion, as we become more attuned to the experiences of those around us. Ultimately, active listening is a powerful tool for cultivating empathy, and for building genuine connections in a world that can often feel disconnected and isolating.

8.5 Empathy in Online Interactions: Challenges and Opportunities

Empathy in online interactions is a critical component of building genuine connections in the digital age. However, it can be challenging to cultivate empathy in virtual spaces due to a lack of nonverbal cues and the anonymity of the internet. This digital disconnect can lead to a breakdown in communication and misunderstanding, making it difficult for individuals to understand and respect each other's perspectives.

The digital age presents unique opportunities for empathy, including the ability to connect with people from diverse backgrounds and experiences. This diversity allows individuals to gain a broader perspective and understanding of different cultures and viewpoints. Furthermore, empathy can be enhanced through active listening and seeking to understand the other person's point of view. Online platforms such as social media and forums can provide a space for individuals to engage in meaningful conversations and gain new insights.

However, empathy in online interactions also faces significant challenges. The anonymity of the internet can lead to aggressive and hostile behavior, making it challenging to engage in respectful communication. The lack of nonverbal cues can also lead to misunderstandings and misinterpretations. Additionally, the echo chamber effect can lead to individuals only engaging with people who share similar beliefs and perspectives, limiting their ability to cultivate empathy and understand diverse viewpoints.

In conclusion, empathy in online interactions is vital for building genuine connections in the digital age. While there are challenges to cultivating empathy in virtual spaces, there are also opportunities to gain new perspectives and engage in meaningful conversations. By actively listening and seeking to understand others' perspectives, individuals can create a more empathetic and connected online community.

8.6 Cultivating Compassion: Understanding the Differences Between Empathy and Sympathy

Cultivating compassion is a vital part of building genuine connections in today's world. However, it's essential to understand the difference between empathy and sympathy to develop compassion effectively. Empathy is the ability to understand and share the feelings of another person. It allows you to put yourself in someone else's shoes and experience their emotions. On the other hand, sympathy means feeling sorry for someone's pain or discomfort but not necessarily understanding or sharing their feelings.

In the digital age, it's easy to confuse empathy with sympathy. We often come across posts, pictures, or videos on social media that evoke our emotions, and we react to them with a quick like or comment. However, these quick reactions are often sympathy rather than empathy. It's crucial to take the time to understand someone's feelings and experiences to develop empathy genuinely.

To cultivate empathy, we need to listen actively, observe body language, and ask questions to gain a deeper understanding of someone's situation. It's also essential to resist the urge to judge or offer solutions immediately, as this can prevent us from fully empathizing with another person's experience.

In conclusion, cultivating compassion requires a deeper understanding of empathy and sympathy. Developing empathy takes time, patience, and a willingness to listen and understand the experiences of others. It's essential to cultivate empathy to build genuine connections and understand and respect others in a digital age.

8.7 Empathy and Social Justice: Using Technology to Build Understanding and Create Change

Empathy and social justice are crucial components for a healthy and peaceful society. Technology has the power to bring people together and create a platform for empathy and understanding. This technology can be used to build bridges between individuals and communities that have been historically divided. By using technology to create empathy and promote social justice, we can work towards a more equitable and just society.

In today's digital age, social media has become a powerful tool for advocacy and social justice. Social media campaigns have the potential to reach millions of people, creating a platform for change. Through social media, individuals and organizations can raise awareness of social issues and promote social justice initiatives. Additionally, social media can connect individuals from different parts of the world and allow them to share their experiences and perspectives.

Technology can also be used to create virtual reality experiences that promote empathy and understanding. Virtual reality experiences can simulate experiences of marginalized communities, allowing individuals to experience and understand their struggles. This technology can be used to build empathy and understanding between individuals and communities that may have different perspectives.

Finally, technology can be used to create online communities that promote social justice and empathy. Through online forums and social media groups, individuals can connect with like-minded individuals to discuss social issues and promote change. These online communities can provide a safe space for individuals to learn, grow, and take action towards promoting social justice.

In conclusion, technology has the power to create empathy and promote social justice. Through social media campaigns, virtual reality experiences, and online communities, individuals can connect with others and work towards a more equitable and just society. It is important that we utilize technology to build bridges and promote empathy, understanding, and respect in a world of digital distractions.

9. Navigating Conflict: Managing Disagreements in a Digitally Connected World

9.1 Understanding Conflict: Types and Triggers

Conflict is a common occurrence in any social situation, and it can take many forms, including verbal, emotional, and physical. It can arise from a variety of sources, such as differences in values, beliefs, opinions, and interests. In the digital age, conflicts can occur more frequently and instantaneously, given the ease and speed of communication through social media and other online platforms. Therefore, it is important to recognize the types and triggers of conflict to manage disagreements effectively and build genuine connections.

One type of conflict is task-related conflict, which occurs when people have differing goals, priorities, or methods of achieving a common objective. For example, two colleagues may disagree on the best approach to complete a project, leading to tension and frustration. Another type of conflict is relationship-related conflict, which arises from personal differences, such as personality clashes, communication styles, or past grievances. For instance, two friends may argue over a misunderstanding or a perceived betrayal, causing hurt and anger.

The triggers of conflict can be internal or external. Internal triggers stem from personal factors, such as emotions, values, and beliefs, that affect how people perceive and react to situations. External triggers can come from environmental factors, such as competition, scarcity, or change, that influence people's behavior and decisions. For example, a disagreement over a political issue may stem from different ideologies and emotional attachments to certain values. On the other hand, a conflict over a limited resource, such as a parking space, may result from the scarcity of available options.

In conclusion, understanding the types and triggers of conflict is essential for navigating disagreements in a digitally connected world. By recognizing the root causes of conflict and developing effective communication and conflict resolution skills, individuals can build genuine connections and maintain positive relationships.

9.2 The Impact of Technology on Conflict Resolution

Technology has drastically changed the way we navigate conflict and manage disagreements in our digitally connected world. With the advent of social media, emails, texting, and instant messaging, conflict resolution can now happen in real-time and without the need for face-to-face interactions. However, the impact of technology on conflict resolution is not all positive.

On the one hand, technology has made communication easier and more accessible, which can lead to quicker and more efficient resolution of conflicts. For instance, online dispute resolution platforms can help parties in conflict come to an agreement without the need for lengthy court proceedings. Additionally, social media can create a space for people to engage in constructive conversations about issues that they may not have been able to address otherwise.

On the other hand, technology can also make conflict resolution more challenging. For example, the anonymity that comes with online communication can lead to trolling, hate speech, and cyberbullying, which can escalate conflicts rather than resolve them. Moreover, the lack of nonverbal cues in digital communication can lead to misunderstandings and misinterpretations, making it harder to come to a resolution.

In conclusion, technology has undoubtedly had an impact on conflict resolution, and we must learn to navigate this impact to ensure that our digital interactions remain constructive and promote genuine connections. While technology can help us resolve conflicts more efficiently, we must also be aware of the challenges that it presents and work to mitigate their negative effects. Ultimately, the key to effective conflict resolution in a digitally connected world is to maintain open communication, active listening, and empathy, regardless of the medium used.

9.3 Online Disagreements: Navigating Trolls and Toxicity

Online disagreements can be a challenging and exhausting experience. With the rise of social media, the prevalence of trolls and toxicity has become more apparent than ever before. Trolls are individuals who intentionally provoke and disrupt online conversations, while toxicity refers to negative and harmful behavior that can escalate quickly. Navigating these types of situations can be overwhelming, but there are some strategies that you can use to manage disagreements effectively.

Firstly, it is important to recognize the signs of toxic behavior and to disengage when necessary. This could mean muting or blocking individuals who are targeting you or simply taking a break from social media altogether. Secondly, it is essential to remain calm and avoid reacting impulsively to negative comments or messages. Taking time to reflect on your response and seeking advice from a trusted friend or mentor can help you to respond thoughtfully and constructively.

Another effective strategy is to focus on building genuine connections with others online. This involves actively seeking out individuals who share similar interests or values and engaging in meaningful conversations with them. By creating a positive and supportive online community, you are less likely to encounter trolls and toxicity and more likely to build genuine friendships and connections.

In conclusion, navigating online disagreements can be challenging, but it is possible to manage effectively with the right strategies. By recognizing toxic behavior, remaining calm and measured in your responses, and focusing on building genuine connections, you can create a positive online environment that fosters authentic human connections.

9.4 The Importance of Active Listening in Conflict Resolution

Conflict is an inevitable part of human interaction, especially in today's digitally connected world where communication happens almost instantaneously. However, the key to resolving conflicts lies in active listening. Active listening involves paying attention to what the other person is saying, understanding their perspective, and responding appropriately. When we actively listen, we not only gain a deeper understanding of the situation, but we also show respect for the other person's thoughts and feelings.

Active listening is particularly important in conflict resolution because it enables both parties to express their concerns and work towards a mutually acceptable solution. It allows for empathy and compassion to be shown, as both parties can better understand each other's point of view. This, in turn, helps to build trust and strengthen relationships. Furthermore, active listening helps to prevent misunderstandings and promotes clear communication, reducing the likelihood of future conflicts.

When we listen actively, we give the other person space to express themselves fully, and we do not interrupt, judge, or dismiss their feelings or ideas. We remain present in the moment and show genuine interest in their perspective. This approach creates a safe and respectful environment for both parties to engage in an honest and productive conversation.

In conclusion, active listening is a crucial element of conflict resolution. It allows for better communication, empathy, and understanding, ultimately leading to stronger relationships and more effective solutions. By practicing active listening, we can build genuine connections with others and navigate conflicts in a digitally connected world with greater ease.

9.5 Finding Common Ground: Strategies for Compromise

In today's digitally connected world, conflicts and disagreements are common. It is essential to find common ground to resolve these conflicts and achieve a compromise. One strategy for finding common ground is to identify the shared values and goals of the parties involved. By recognizing these commonalities, it can be easier to work towards a resolution that satisfies everyone involved.

Another strategy is to actively listen to the other party's perspective. When people feel heard and understood, they are more likely to be open to finding a compromise. It is important to avoid interrupting, dismissing, or belittling the other person's perspective. Instead, ask questions to clarify their viewpoint and show empathy towards their concerns.

A third strategy is to focus on the problem rather than the person. Personal attacks and insults only escalate conflicts and make it harder to find a compromise. By shifting the focus to the issue at hand, it is easier to come up with solutions that benefit everyone involved.

Finally, it is important to be willing to give something up in order to reach a compromise. Compromise requires both parties to make concessions and find a middle ground. This may mean letting go of some of your own demands or finding creative solutions that meet everyone's needs.

In summary, finding common ground and achieving a compromise in a digitally connected world requires identifying shared values, active listening, focusing on the problem, and being willing to make concessions. By using these strategies, it is possible to navigate conflicts and disagreements in a way that builds genuine connections and fosters mutual understanding.

9.6 The Role of Emotional Intelligence in Conflict Resolution

The ability to manage emotions and understand the emotions of others is known as emotional intelligence (EI). In conflict resolution, EI plays a critical role in navigating disagreements and finding solutions that benefit all parties involved. When individuals have high levels of EI, they can remain calm and level-headed in tense situations, which can help de-escalate conflicts. Additionally, they can empathize with others and understand their perspectives, which can lead to more effective communication and collaboration.

One of the key components of EI is self-awareness, or the ability to recognize and understand one's emotions. When individuals are self-aware, they can identify their triggers and manage their responses. For example, if someone is feeling frustrated or angry during a conflict, they can take a step back and reflect on why they feel that way before reacting. This can help them communicate effectively and avoid saying or doing things they may later regret.

Another important aspect of EI in conflict resolution is empathy. When individuals are able to put themselves in someone else's shoes and understand their perspective, it can help build trust and create a more collaborative environment. By acknowledging and validating the other person's feelings and concerns, individuals can work together to find a mutually beneficial solution.

Overall, EI is a critical skill in conflict resolution. By managing emotions and understanding the emotions of others, individuals can communicate effectively, build trust, and find solutions that benefit everyone involved. In a digitally connected world where disagreements are unavoidable, developing strong emotional intelligence is more important than ever.

9.7 De-escalating Conflict: Tips for Managing Intense Situations

In today's digitally connected world, conflicts arise more frequently than ever before. It is essential to know how to handle intense situations and de-escalate them before they get out of hand. If left unaddressed, conflicts can have devastating effects on relationships and lead to mental and emotional stress. Here are some tips for managing intense situations and de-escalating conflicts:

1. Stay Calm: When faced with a conflict, it is crucial to remain calm and composed. Take a few deep breaths, and try to focus on your thoughts and emotions.

2. Listen: Listen to the other person's point of view without interrupting or judging them. Listening shows that you value their opinion and are willing to work towards a solution.

3. Acknowledge: Acknowledge the other person's feelings and needs. This helps to build empathy and shows that you understand their perspective.

4. Reframe: Reframe the situation by finding common ground. A shared goal can help redirect the conversation towards finding a solution.

5. Collaborate: Work together to find a solution that works for everyone. Collaboration helps to build trust and strengthens relationships.

6. Apologize: If you are at fault, apologize sincerely. Apologizing shows that you take responsibility for your actions and that you value the other person's feelings.

In conclusion, conflicts are a part of life, and it is essential to know how to handle them. De-escalating conflicts can prevent them from escalating and causing more significant damage. By staying calm, listening, acknowledging, reframing, collaborating, and apologizing, you can manage intense situations and build stronger relationships.

9.8 Apologizing and Forgiveness: Repairing Relationships After Conflict

Apologizing and forgiveness are two essential elements in repairing relationships after conflict. Conflict can arise in any relationship, and it is important to understand that it is normal and even healthy to have disagreements. However, what sets healthy relationships apart from those that are not is the ability to navigate and resolve conflicts effectively.

When conflicts occur, both parties may feel the need to defend themselves, which can escalate the situation. Apologizing can help to de-escalate the situation by acknowledging the other person's feelings, taking responsibility for one's actions, and expressing remorse for any harm caused. A sincere apology can go a long way in repairing a damaged relationship.

However, it is also important to understand that apologizing does not automatically lead to forgiveness. Forgiveness is a personal process that the offended party must undertake. It involves letting go of anger, resentment, and the desire for revenge. Forgiveness does not mean forgetting or excusing the behavior that caused the conflict, but rather releasing oneself from the negative emotions associated with it.

In a digitally connected world, conflict can arise more frequently due to the ease of communication and the potential for misunderstandings. However, the same principles of apologizing and forgiveness still apply. It is important to communicate openly and directly, to listen actively, and to approach conflicts with a willingness to understand the other person's point of view.

In conclusion, conflict is a natural part of relationships, but it is essential to approach it with a mindset of repair rather than destruction. Apologizing and forgiveness are two crucial elements in repairing relationships after conflict, and they require a willingness to take responsibility and let go of negative emotions. By navigating conflict effectively, we can build genuine connections even in a world of digital distractions.

9.9 Moving Forward: Learning from Conflict and Building Stronger Connections

Managing disagreements and conflict is an inevitable part of building genuine connections, especially in a digitally connected world where communication is often mediated by technology. But the key to navigating conflict is not to avoid it altogether, but to learn from it and use it as an opportunity to build stronger connections. This requires a willingness to listen, empathize, and understand the perspectives of others, even when they differ from our own.

One way to do this is to practice active listening, which involves fully engaging with the speaker and trying to understand their point of view, rather than simply waiting for our turn to speak. This can help to reduce misunderstandings and defensiveness, and foster a deeper sense of connection and understanding.

Another important part of managing conflict is to avoid making assumptions or jumping to conclusions based on limited information. In a world where much of our communication is digital and therefore lacks the nuances of face-to-face interaction, it's easy to misinterpret tone, intent, and meaning. Taking the time to clarify our understanding and ask questions can help to prevent misunderstandings and build trust.

Finally, it's important to be willing to compromise and find common ground, even if we don't agree on everything. This requires a willingness to put our egos aside and prioritize the relationship over being right or winning an argument. By doing this, we can build stronger, more resilient connections that can withstand the inevitable disagreements and conflicts that arise in any relationship.

In short, learning from conflict and building stronger connections requires a commitment to active listening, avoiding assumptions, and being willing to compromise. By embracing these principles, we can navigate disagreements in a way that strengthens our connections and helps us build more genuine, meaningful relationships in a world of digital distractions.

10. Conclusion: Finding Balance and Building Lasting Connections in a Technology-Driven Society

10.1 The Effects of Technology on Connection

The effects of technology on connection are a complex issue in today's society. While technology has made communication more convenient and accessible, it has also created a sense of disconnection and isolation. Social media platforms, for instance, have made it easier for people to connect with others, but they have also created a sense of competition and comparison among individuals. As people spend more time on their devices, they become less engaged with their immediate surroundings and the people around them.

Moreover, technology has made it easier for people to avoid face-to-face conversations and confrontations. It has also created a sense of anonymity, making it easier for people to say things online that they would not say in person. This can lead to misunderstandings and conflicts, further eroding genuine connections.

However, technology can also be used to strengthen connections. Video conferencing, for example, can allow people to have face-to-face conversations with loved ones who live far away. Social media can also be used to connect with like-minded individuals and build communities. Nevertheless, it is important to maintain a balance between the use of technology and personal interactions.

In conclusion, technology has both positive and negative effects on connection. It is important to be mindful of how much time we spend on our devices and to make an effort to connect with the people around us. By finding a balance between technology and personal interaction, we can build lasting connections in a technology-driven society.

10.2 The Importance of Balance in a Technology-Driven Society

In today's society, technology has become an integral part of our lives. It has changed the way we communicate, work, and even entertain ourselves. However, with the increased dependence on technology, there is a risk of losing balance in our lives. It is crucial to maintain balance and use technology in a way that enhances our lives, rather than becoming a hindrance.

Maintaining balance means finding the right mix of technology and human interaction. With the rise of social media and messaging apps, it has become easy to connect with people digitally. However, it is essential to remember the value of face-to-face communication. Our brains are wired to pick up on body language and other nonverbal cues, which are often lost in digital communication. Real human interaction is vital for building genuine connections and maintaining relationships.

Another aspect of balance is managing the time spent on technology. It is easy to get lost in the endless scroll of social media or binge-watch shows on streaming platforms. However, it is crucial to set boundaries and limit the time spent on technology. This allows us to prioritize other aspects of our lives, such as our hobbies or spending time with loved ones.

In conclusion, finding balance in a technology-driven society is essential for building genuine connections and leading a fulfilling life. It is important to remember the value of face-to-face communication and manage the time spent on technology. By finding the right balance, we can use technology to enhance our lives and build lasting connections.

10.3 Finding Meaningful Connection in a Digital Age

In today's digital age, it's easy to feel disconnected from others in spite of being constantly connected online. The allure of social media platforms and the instant gratification they offer can easily become a substitute for genuine human connection, leaving us feeling unfulfilled and lonely. However, it's important to remember that technology is a tool, and it's up to us to use it in a way that enhances our lives rather than detracts from them.

To find meaningful connections in a digital age, we need to be intentional in our interactions online and offline. It's essential to carve out time for face-to-face conversations with loved ones and to make an effort to truly listen and engage with them. Additionally, we can seek out online communities that align with our interests and values, and actively participate in discussions and events. This not only allows us to connect with like-minded individuals but also provides opportunities for personal growth and learning.

It's also important to be mindful of our social media use and the impact it has on our mental health. Logging off for extended periods and taking breaks from scrolling can help us stay present and focused on building genuine connections with those around us. Finally, we need to remember that building meaningful connections takes time and effort. It's not something that can be rushed or achieved through a few clicks of a button. By prioritizing genuine human connection and being intentional in our interactions, we can build lasting relationships that enrich our lives and bring us fulfillment.

10.4 The Power of Intentionality in Building Lasting Connections

In today's fast-paced society, building lasting connections has become more challenging than ever before. With the rise of technology and social media, individuals are often more connected digitally than in person. However, the power of intentionality can help individuals build genuine, long-lasting connections in a world of constant digital distractions.

Intentionality refers to the deliberate act of thoughtfully choosing one's actions and words to achieve a specific outcome. When it comes to building relationships, being intentional means actively seeking out opportunities to connect with others and making a conscious effort to nurture those relationships over time. This can involve scheduling regular catch-ups with friends, sending thoughtful messages to loved ones, or even reaching out to new people with similar interests.

By being intentional in our relationships, we can foster deeper connections with others that extend beyond surface-level interactions. Genuine connections require a mutual investment of time, effort, and emotional energy, something that cannot be achieved through a quick Facebook message or Instagram DM. Instead, it requires consistent and intentional action to build trust and rapport with others.

In a world that is increasingly reliant on technology to connect, cultivating genuine relationships requires a conscious effort to disconnect from the digital world and focus on building authentic connections in real life. By recognizing the power of intentionality, individuals can build lasting connections that enrich their lives and bring them closer to the people they care about the most.

10.5 The Future of Connection: Navigating Technology and Relationships

The future of connection is a complex and constantly evolving landscape. As technology continues to advance and shape our world, it is important that we navigate the intersection of technology and relationships with care and intentionality. While technology has the potential to bring us closer together, it can also create barriers and distractions that prevent us from building genuine connections. As we move forward, it is important that we find ways to balance the benefits of technology with the need for human connection.

One key aspect of navigating the future of connection is cultivating mindfulness and intentionality in our use of technology. By being aware of the ways in which technology can impact our relationships, we can make conscious choices about how we use it and prioritize human connection. This might mean setting aside time to disconnect from technology and focus on in-person interactions, or being mindful of the ways in which social media and other platforms can influence our perceptions and interactions with others.

Another important aspect of navigating the future of connection is recognizing the role that technology can play in building and sustaining relationships. From social media to dating apps, technology has created new avenues for connecting with others and finding meaningful relationships. However, it is important to approach these platforms with a critical eye and recognize the limitations of virtual interactions. Ultimately, building lasting connections requires a willingness to be vulnerable, communicate openly, and prioritize the needs and feelings of others.

As we navigate the future of connection, it is clear that technology will continue to shape the way we interact with each other. However, by approaching technology with mindfulness and intentionality, we can build lasting connections that are grounded in genuine human connection.

Printed in Great Britain
by Amazon

26320251R00076